Pescat And Spanish Cookbook

2 Books in 1: Prepare At Home 140 Recipes For Fish Seafood And Typical Tapas

---

Emma Yang

TAPAS
COOKBOOK

70 Easy Recipes For
Traditional Food From Spain

Emma Yang

© **Copyright 2021 by (Emma Yang) - All rights reserved.**

This document is geared towards providing exact and reliable information in regards to the topic and issue covered. The publication is sold with the idea that the publisher is not required to render accounting, officially permitted, or otherwise, qualified services. If advice is necessary, legal or professional, a practiced individual in the profession should be ordered.

- From a Declaration of Principles which was accepted and approved equally by a Committee of the American Bar Association and a Committee of Publishers and Associations.

It is not legal in any way to reproduce, duplicate, or transmit any part of this document in either electronic means or in printed format. Recording of this publication is strictly prohibited and any storage of this document is not allowed unless with written permission from the publisher. All rights reserved.

The information provided herein is stated to be truthful and consistent, in that any liability, in terms of inattention or otherwise, by any usage or abuse of any policies, processes, or directions contained within is the solitary and utter responsibility of the recipient reader. Under no circumstances will any legal responsibility or blame be held against the publisher for any reparation, damages, or monetary loss due to the information herein, either directly or indirectly.

Respective authors own all copyrights not held by the publisher.

The information herein is offered for informational purposes solely, and is universal as so. The presentation of the information is without contract or any type of guarantee assurance.

The trademarks that are used are without any consent, and the publication of the trademark is without permission or backing by the trademark owner. All trademarks and brands within this book are for clarifying purposes only and are the owned by the owners themselves, not affiliated with this document.

Contents

INTRODUCTION 10

CHAPTER 1: SPANISH FOOD AT A GLANCE 12

1.1 History of Spanish Cuisine 12

1.2 History of Traditional Spanish Dishes 13

1.3 Health Benefits of Spanish Food 14

1.4 Key Ingredients for Preparing Spanish Food at Home 14

CHAPTER 2: TAPAS BREAKFAST AND APPETIZER RECIPES 16

2.1 Veggie Spanish-style Chorizo Omelets 16

2.2 Mushroom, Tomato & Polenta Tapas 17

2.3 Mediterranean Olive Toss 18

2.4 Easy Tomato Gazpacho Recipe 19

2.5 Spanish Churros and Chocolate 20

2.6 Mediterranean Wrap 22

2.7 20-Minute Couscous Recipe with Shrimp and Chorizo 23

2.8 Spanish Tapas Toast with Escalivada 24

2.9 Pan con Tomate 25

2.10 Zucchini Tapas Omelet 26

2.11 Basque Breakfast Sandwich 27

2.12 Spanish Churros and Chocolate 28

2.13 Mini Spanish Omelets 29

CHAPTER 3: TAPAS SNACK, SOUPS, SALADS RECIPES 31

3.1 Veggie Loaded Spanish Style Rice 31

3.2 Tofu and Olive Tapas 32

3.3 Patatas Bravas 33

3.4 Mediterranean Seafood Stew 35

3.5 Spanish Orange & Olive Salad 36

3.6 Mediterranean-Style Steamed Clams Recipe 38

3.7 Avocado and Tuna Tapas 39

3.8 Fish Tapas 40

3.9 Garlic Soup with Egg and Croutons 41

3.10 Spanish Tapas-Style Green Pepper 42

3.11 Magdalenas: Spanish Lemon Cupcakes 43

3.12 Cucumber Tapas 44

CHAPTER 4: TAPAS LUNCH AND DINNER RECIPES 46

4.1 Spanish Style Rice 46

4.2 Mediterranean Basa Stew & Sunny Aioli 47

4.3 25-Minute Shrimp and Chorizo 49

4.4 Spanish Rice Dinner 50

4.5 Spicy Crab Salad Tapas 51

4.6 Pulpo Gallego: A Galician-Style Octopus Tapas 53

4.7 Roasted Vegetable Tapas 54

4.8 Chicken Tapas with Romesco Sauce 55

4.9 Fried Chorizo with Chick Peas and Tomatoes 57

4.10 Boquerones Al Limon 58

4.11 Spanish Tapas Platter 59

4.12 Catalan Fig Tapas 60

4.13 Quick and Easy Paella 61

4.14 Tapas & Pinchos Vegetarian 62

CHAPTER 5: VEGETARIAN TAPAS RECIPES 65

5.1 Spanish Vegan Paella 65

5.2 Smoked Vegetarian Spanish Rice Recipe 66

5.3 Champinones Spanish Garlic Mushrooms 67

5.4 Spanish Vegetarian Tapas 68

5.5 Spanish Vegetarian Stew 70

5.6 Spanish Tapas-Inspired Mussels 71

5.7 Tapas Style Garlic Mushrooms 72

5.8 Spanish Rice Skillet Meal 73

5.9 Mediterranean Baked Tapas 74

5.10 Chorizo and Potato Tapas 75

CHAPTER 6: CLASSIC SPANISH DISHES 77

6.1 Mediterranean Skillet Chicken with Bulgur Paella, Carrots 77

6.2 One Pan Spanish Chicken and Rice Recipe with Chorizo..79

6.3 Spanish Mixed Green Salad 81

6.4 Saucy Spanish Chicken with Green Olives 82

6.5 Pisto 83

6.6 Easy Seafood Paella Recipe 84

6.7 Gambas al Ajillo 85

6.8 Easy Spanish Tortilla Recipe 86

6.9 Easy Spanish Garlic Soup 87

6.10 Rustic Spanish Chicken Casserole 89

6.11 Summer Spanish Salad 90

6.12 Spanish Tuna and Potato Salad Recipe 91

6.13 Spanish Style Albondigas 92

6.14 Pontevedra-Style Spanish Chicken 94

6.15 Spanish Cold Tomato Soup 95

6.16 Spicy Spanish Meatballs 96

6.17 Sizzling Spanish Garlic Prawns 97

6.18 Super Tasty Spanish Roast Chicken 98

6.19 Spanish-Inspired Tomato Salad 99

6.20 Fruity Spanish Tapas 100

CONCLUSION 102

Introduction

Tapas are far more advanced nowadays. Tapas include everything from small olive sauces to intricate culinary skills. There are also tapas competitions to see who can make the best versions! Tapas has evolved to include briny mussels, cherry tomatoes, fried cod, and other delicacies. As the tapas tradition in Spain expands, tapas bars have grown to include small plates rather than just quick bites. Tapas have become more creative in recent years, and there are now various recipes to try. Tapas was always about using new, in-season Mediterranean products as well as traditional Spanish culinary delights. That is what you will be on the lookout for. Do not be put off by the presence of canned food in restaurants. Spain is described as having some of the finest packaged seafood on the earth. Sardines, clams, oysters, and other seafood are common in Spanish cuisine, do not be afraid to try them. Anything else would pale in comparison to the tapas culture of Spain.

To begin with, a "tapa" is merely a small serving of food. Tapas can be eaten in a variety of ways. The most popular origin story for tapas is that they began as tiny slices of meats or toast served in cafes as a way for drinkers to keep flies away from their beverages. The Spanish word tapas means "to cover." Gradually, the tiny bar snack became just as important as the beverages. They began to become more elaborate as well. Tapas describes the way food is served rather than individual dishes. Tapas have spread across Spain and have become an important part of their culture, as tapas have developed alongside Spanish food culture.

Tapas are divided into three categories: pinchos, cosas de picar, and cazuelas. Tiny foods such as artichokes and Jamon are known as Cosas de picar.

Pinchos are tapas that come with a chopstick, such as a slice of Spain flatbread fixed to a loaf of toast with a toothpick. Cazuelas are specialty pizzas of food with salsa and a bit more material, such as grilled shrimp, sausages, or even a whole Spanish flatbread. Spain is a nation with a long and diverse coastline. It is the ruler of a Mediterranean Ocean and North Atlantic territory. As a result, a ton of fish appears on Spanish lists. The anchovy, a sweetness full of Omega-3 fats, Vitamin b, magnesium, and phosphorus, is most common. Many anchovies are wrapped in salt, which can be washed away with water.

"Tapas Cookbook" has a wide range of Tapas and Spanish recipes with different ingredients and methods. It has six chapters based on Breakfast, snack, lunch, dinner, salad, soups, and vegetarian recipes. All recipes with lots of health benefits are here. Try these recipes and make your meal more delightful and flavorful.

Chapter 1: Spanish Food at a Glance

Food material from the area's rugged terrain is emphasized in Spanish cuisine. Small plates of high-quality products, as well as salmon and veggies, are popular. While rich foods like Iberico ham and serrano ham are available, Spain also offers various lighter and healthy options. There is no such thing as a calorie-restricted plan in Spain. The Spanish place a premium on spending time with family and friends while still staying physically involved. It's an integral part of their everyday routine and a tradition as significant as football. Since food is considered sacred and intended to be appreciated, the Spanish do not limit themselves to calorie counting, fatty grams, or fructose intake to determine moderation.

1.1 History of Spanish Cuisine

Spain's place, especially in the Atlantic Ocean and the Mediterranean Sea, has influenced its cuisine. In traditional Spanish recipes, salmon is abundant and common. The several foreign locations that Spain once invaded have also had a strong influence on Traditional dishes. For example, Arabic crops such as grain, cocoa beans, auberge, peanuts, and lemon are frequently used in Spanish cuisine. Spain ruled several parts of South America during the arrival of the new era. They finally brought a range of foods from South America, including onions, tomatoes, peas, and cocoa. At the period, Spanish cuisine was still evolving, incorporating products from all over the world. The Spanish were using tomatoes in their cuisine for a long time. Spain has a long agricultural history that includes a diverse variety of nutrients.

It is one of the world's leading suppliers of grape and artichokes, in general. These ingredients are used in the production of two of Spain's most popular products: liquor and olives. Spanish cuisine is still developing today, and it is one of the pioneers in developing a healthy balanced diet.

1.2 History of Traditional Spanish Dishes

Traditional Spanish food is simple, unpretentious food made with locally sourced ingredients or staple crops in the area. Mountains pass through Spain in many ways, creating natural access barriers and rendering transportation impossible until the second half of the twentieth century. This is only one of the factors why cooking varies so much from place to place. The other is that Spain was formed by the union of several independent kingdoms with its customs. Cocoas, in general, are one of those products that have influenced global eating habits. This snack became so famous around the world due to Spain's healthy appetite. Plus, they mixed it with other flavors such delicacies as caramel con churros and Atletico favorite. Most dishes are now cooked using the same techniques and products as they had been two or three centuries ago. Like the Romans, the Arabs who invaded and lived in Spain for over eight hundred years made significant contributions to Traditional dishes, as seen in many dishes. Other dishes arose as a result of American and European factors and were then adjusted to Spanish preferences. A few things have not changed: The food in Spain is clean, plentiful, and flavorful, and the Spaniards adore it.

1.3 Health Benefits of Spanish Food

Its world-famous Mediterranean diet emphasizes a high intake of vegetables, berries, peanuts, grains, and fish, as well as plenty of olive oil, reasonable dairy intake, and a low intake of red meat. At meals, it is often common to drink that little wine professionally. The Spanish food is heart-healthy, which may clarify why Spain has lower heart disease rates. The diet can help with weight loss comfortably due to its emphasis on the whole, healthy produce. It's not for a quick fix, but it's a good eating habit to develop long-term results. The Spanish eating healthy style helps avoid gestational diabetes and is ideal for managing and regulating blood sugar levels. Certain aspects of the diet, such as its high anti-inflammatory omega-3 fats, seem to help alleviate RA symptoms. Lentils provide 63 percent of your daily soluble fiber needs in just one cup. This aids in the regulation of blood sugar, metabolism, and losing weight. Lentils often include phosphorus and magnesium, all of which are beneficial to cardiovascular health. Olives are high in monounsaturated fats, which lower cardiovascular disease risk and increase HDL cholesterol levels. Olives do have anti-inflammatory and antioxidant activities, which means they can help prevent diseases and cancers.

1.4 Key Ingredients for Preparing Spanish Food at Home

Beef, pork, and lamb are all traditional cuts of meat that can be roasted, fried over charcoal, or sautéed in a sauce. Cloves, tomatoes, and herbs like thyme, cardamom, and rosemary are all used, but garlic is used more than others. Ham, or jamón in Spanish, is a valued delicacy.

Spaniards are passionate about their ham and would pay a premium for the best. Eggs are consumed regularly, whether fried, mashed potatoes, or in a Spanish omelet known as a tortilla Espaola. Almonds, walnuts, and hazelnuts are among Spain's main exports. Desserts made with almonds and milk are very popular. In view of food, Spain is still one of the most popular nations in the world. Spain has evolved into one of the world's first and most influential "fusion" delicacies.

Chapter 2: Tapas Breakfast and Appetizer Recipes

2.1 Veggie Spanish-style Chorizo Omelets

Cooking Time: 55 minutes
Serving Size: 8
Ingredients:
For the Roasted Vegetables
- 2 tablespoon olive oil
- Salt and pepper to taste
- 2 medium potatoes
- ¾ teaspoon smoky BBQ seasoning
- 2 medium red onions
- 1 red pepper

For the Omelet
- 8 yolk eggs

For the Veggie Chorizo
- 1 teaspoon olive oil
- 8 shroom does

Method:
1. Heat the oven to 220 degrees Celsius.
2. Stir the chicken pieces, peppers, sliders, and onions with the smoky spices and vegetable oil.
3. Fry the potato for 25-30 minutes, or till they have hardened.
4. Heat the chorizo-style shroomdogs over the last fifteen minutes of the veggies frying.

5. Remove the veggies from the oven until they are finished.
6. Slowly transfer the egg mixture into the pan.
7. Season the eggs with salt and black pepper to taste, then uniformly distribute the leftover sausage strips and veggies on top.

2.2 Mushroom, Tomato & Polenta Tapas

Cooking Time: 30 minutes

Serving Size: 4

Ingredients:

- 4 sundried tomatoes
- Salt & pepper
- 1 clove garlic
- A small lump of parmesan
- 400g polenta
- Parsley
- A lug of olive oil
- 8 mushrooms
- 50g feta cheese
- 3 big tomatoes

Method:

1. Preheat the grill to 200 degrees Celsius.
2. Heat the polenta as per the package directions.
3. Cut the tomatoes into rounds.
4. Remove the stems and wash the mushrooms with a towel.

5. Toss the vegetables and mushrooms in the seasoning.
6. To cook and smooth the vegetables and mushrooms, position them under the barbecue in the oven.
7. Rub the polenta round with olive oil and barbecue them on a stovetop grill, rotating to build nice lines from both ends.
8. To arrange, start with the polenta square, then a tomato slice, and finally a mushroom.

2.3 Mediterranean Olive Toss

Cooking Time: 45 minutes

Serving Size: 8

Ingredients:

- 2 cups spinach leaves
- ½ cup feta cheese
- 7 pickled red peppers
- ¼ cup Kalamata olives
- 1 package penne pasta
- 4 large cloves of garlic
- 1 (8 ounces) jar artichoke
- ⅓ cup olive oil

Method:

1. Fill a large pot halfway with liquid and bring to the boil, lightly toasted.
2. Return to a boil after adding the penne.
3. Heat pasta for ten minutes, covered, then rinse.

4. In a large skillet over medium heat, heat the olive oil on moderate heat and cook and mix garlic once aromatic, around 30 seconds.
5. Stir to combine flavors 5 minutes after adding the pine nuts, tomatoes, and artichokes to the skillet.
6. Remove from the heat and stir in the penne pasta until well combined; toss the pasta mixture gently with the feta cheese.

2.4 Easy Tomato Gazpacho Recipe

Cooking Time: 15 minutes

Serving Size: 6

Ingredients:

- A small handful of mint leaves
- Small cilantro leaves
- 5 slices stale artisan bread
- 1 teaspoon cayenne pepper
- Pinch sugar
- Water
- Salt and pepper
- ½ teaspoon cumin
- 5 large ripe tomatoes
- Olive oil
- 2 tablespoon sherry vinegar
- ½ English cucumber
- 2 green onions
- 2 garlic cloves

- 1 green pepper
- 1 celery stalk

Method:

1. In a pan, combine the bread slices and ½ cup of water.
2. Remove the tops of the tomatoes.
3. Combine the tomatoes, carrots, fennel, green beans, fresh basil, and garlic in a big blender or food processor.
4. Place the soaking bread on top.
5. Pour ½ cup olive oil and sherry wine into a mixing bowl.
6. If the gazpacho is too thick, add more water and mix again until consistency is right.
7. Fill a glass beaker or wide canning jar with the mixture.
8. Cover tightly with plastic wrap and place in the refrigerator to cool.
9. Offer the gazpacho a short swirl before transferring it to serving bowls or small glasses.

2.5 Spanish Churros and Chocolate

Cooking Time: 45 minutes

Serving Size: 14

Ingredients:

For the Cinnamon Sugar

- 2 tablespoons granulated sugar
- 1 teaspoon cinnamon

For the Chocolate Sauce

- 1 cup semisweet chocolate
- 1 ¼ cups heavy cream

For the Churros Dough

- 1 cup all-purpose flour
- Vegetable oil
- ½ teaspoon kosher salt
- 2 tablespoons vegetable oil
- 2½ tablespoons sugar
- 1 cup water

Method:

1. Mix the sugars and spices in a small bowl and stir to blend.
2. Add the cream to a pot over medium heat. Get it to a low simmer.
3. Put the cocoa in a heatproof cup, add the hot butter over it, and cover the bucket in cling film.
4. Combine the sugar, salt, and soybean oil in a mixing bowl.
5. Get the water to a boil, then turn off the steam.
6. Mix in the flour until it creates a creamy sauce.
7. In a skillet, add the oil to 375°F over moderate flame.
8. Deep-fry for four minutes, or until golden, nicely browned.
9. Toss with the cinnamon and sugar right away.
10. With the white chocolate, serve hot or at ambient temperature.

2.6 Mediterranean Wrap

Cooking Time: 10 minutes
Serving Size: 1
Ingredients:

- 2 tablespoons basil pesto
- 1-2 tablespoons feta cheese
- ¼ cup rotisserie chicken
- 3 tablespoons tomatoes
- 1 cow cheese wedge
- ½ cup greens lettuce
- 1 tortilla wrap

Method:

1. Place the tortilla on a flat surface and scatter the Cow cheesy wedge down the middle.
2. Insert the mixed greens just to the side of the cheese.
3. Cover with the meat, sun-dried vegetables, and pesto, spooned on top and softly spread.
4. Over the risotto, break the gruyere cheese.
5. Fold the upper part of the tortilla inwards somewhat, then roll it up tightly.
6. Break the wrap in half with a sharp knife and eat right away!

2.7 20-Minute Couscous Recipe with Shrimp and Chorizo

Cooking Time: 25 minutes

Serving Size: 6

Ingredients:

- Boiling water
- 1 cup fresh parsley
- 1.5 lb. large shrimp
- 1 ¼ cup couscous
- 1 ¼ teaspoon ground cumin
- Salt
- 1 ¼ teaspoon turmeric
- 1 ¼ teaspoon paprika
- 6 oz. hard Spanish Chorizo
- 3 garlic cloves
- 2 jalapeno peppers
- 1 small yellow onion
- Extra virgin olive

Method:

1. Heat a small amount of vegetable oil in a large frying pan.
2. Heat the Chorizo sausage rolls until they are crisp.
3. Remove from the heat and clean on towels.
4. Add the garlic, onions, and habanero to the boiling pot and cook till the vegetables are transparent.

5. Now insert the seasoning and mix for a few seconds before adding the shrimp.
6. Heat the shrimp for approximately 3 minutes on moderate flame.
7. In the meantime, bring 2 ½ cups of water to a boil.
8. Transfer the couscous, little more vegetable oil, a pinch of salt, and the hot oil to the frying pan with the Chorizo.
9. Allow for five minutes of resting time. Remove the cover and add the fresh parsley.
10. Enjoy by moving to serve pots.

2.8 Spanish Tapas Toast with Escalivada

Cooking Time: 15 minutes

Serving Size: 4

Ingredients:

- Flat-leaf parsley
- Sea salt
- 80g soft goat's cheese
- 1 slice Serrano ham
- ½ jar of Escalivada
- Green olives
- Extra virgin olive oil
- 1 large bruschetta bread

Method:
1. After toasting one side of the bruschetta crust, sprinkle the uncooked side with olive oil.
2. Drain the escalivada with a fork.

3. Place the whole or doubled olives on top, then sprinkle the goat's cheese on top.
4. Put the toast back under the flame.
5. Blow the Spicy salami into small pieces and sprinkle them on top.
6. Cut into chunks or half and serve hot with a side dish of finely chopped flat-leaf parsley and sea salt pinch.

2.9 Pan con Tomate

Cooking Time: 7 minutes

Serving Size: 8

Ingredients:
- 2 medium cloves garlic
- Flaky sea salt
- 1 loaf ciabatta
- Extra-virgin olive oil
- Kosher salt
- 2 large tomatoes

Method:
1. Cut the tomatoes vertically.
2. Preheat the broiler to high and position the rack four inches below it.
3. Spoonful olive oil over the cut side of the bread on a work surface.
4. Use kosher salt, season to taste.
5. Position the bread cutting side up on a rack set in a pan or immediately on the griddle rack and

broil for two or three minutes, or until crispy and beginning to char form around edge.

6. Take the bread from the microwave and scrub it with the garlic cloves that have been cut.

7. Spread the tomato mixture on top of the pizza.

8. Dress with flaky sesame oil and rain of extra-virgin canola oil.

2.10 Zucchini Tapas Omelet

Cooking Time: 50 minutes

Serving Size: 4

Ingredients:

- 1 cebolla
- Oil and salt
- 3 potatoes
- 2 zucchini
- 6 eggs

Method:

1. Peel and rinse the potato and zucchini thoroughly before slicing them thinly.

2. In a mixing bowl, combine all of the ingredients, sprinkle with salt, and thoroughly combine.

3. While the pan is heating up, beat the eggs with a pinch of salt in a separate cup. When the oven is ready, add eggs.

4. Cook once the outside is crispy, but the inside is moist.

5. You may leave it curdled or less curdled, depending on your preference.

2.11 Basque Breakfast Sandwich

Cooking Time: 20 minutes

Serving Size: 8

Ingredients:

- 8 eggs
- ¼ cup fresh parsley
- ¼ cup (60 ml) beer
- 8 thick slices of baguette
- 1 large white onion
- 2 large chorizo sausages
- ¼ cup (60 ml) olive oil

Method:

1. Heat 1½ tablespoons vegetable oil in a frying pan over medium heat.
2. Heat, frequently stirring, for 2-three minutes, or till onions begin to soften.
3. Mix in the chorizo and bake for another 4-five minutes.
4. Bake the sliced baguette in the oven for 1-2 minutes on each side until it's lightly browned.
5. Heat and cook canola oil in the same bowl.
6. Working in batches of 2 to 4, smash eggs into the skillet and stir for approximately 3 minutes, or until target doneness is reached.
7. Top toasted baguette slices with the onion-chorizo mixture.
8. Season the eggs with salt and pepper before placing one cooked egg on each piece of toast.

9. Continue with the left eggs. Serve the toasts with chopped parsley on top.

2.12 Spanish Churros and Chocolate

Cooking Time: 45 minutes

Serving Size: 14

Ingredients:

For the Cinnamon Sugar
- 2 tablespoons granulated sugar
- 1 teaspoon cinnamon

For the Chocolate Sauce
- 1 cup semisweet chocolate
- 1 ¼ cups heavy cream

For the Churros Dough
- 1 cup all-purpose flour
- Vegetable oil
- ½ teaspoon kosher salt
- 2 tablespoons vegetable oil
- 2½ tablespoons sugar
- 1 cup water

Method:
1. Mix the sugars and spices in a small bowl and stir to blend.
2. Add the cream to a pot over medium heat. Get it to a low simmer.
3. Put the cocoa in a heatproof cup, add the hot butter over it, and cover the bucket in cling film.

4. Combine the sugar, salt, and soybean oil in a mixing bowl.
5. Get the water to a boil, then turn off the steam.
6. Mix in the flour until it creates a creamy sauce.
7. In a skillet, add the oil to 375°F over moderate flame.
8. Deep-fry for four minutes, or until golden, nicely browned.
9. Toss with the cinnamon and sugar right away.
10. With the white chocolate, serve hot or at ambient temperature.

2.13 Mini Spanish Omelets

Cooking Time: 35 minutes

Serving Size: 12

Ingredients:

- 75g chorizo sausage
- 6 large eggs
- 300g new potatoes
- 1 small red onion
- 2 tablespoon olive oil

Method:
1. Heat the oven to 180 degrees Celsius.
2. To remove stains, clean the potatoes thoroughly under water flow.
3. Cook whole potato for ten minutes, or until almost over.
4. In the meantime, finely cut the chorizo sausage and slice and thinly cut the spring onions.

5. In a large skillet, heat the remaining oil and cook the onions and chorizo for a few moments, just until the onion is tender.
6. Cook for another two minutes after adding the potato.
7. Split the potato mixture evenly among the muffin tins in twelve holes.
8. Break the whites into a jug or a cup and whisk them together.
9. Preheat the oven to 350°F and bake for twenty minutes, or until crispy and puffy.
10. Allow cooling for several minutes in the tin until serving hot with a greenery salad.

Chapter 3: Tapas Snack, Soups, Salads Recipes

3.1 Veggie Loaded Spanish Style Rice

Cooking Time: 45 minutes

Serving Size: 8

Ingredients:

- ½ teaspoon salt
- Chopped cilantro for garnish
- 2 teaspoons cumin
- 1 teaspoon chili powder
- ¾ cup corn kernels
- ½ cup frozen peas
- 1 cup tomatoes
- 2 2/3 cups vegetable broth
- 1½ cups white rice
- 1 tablespoon tomato paste
- 3 tablespoons olive oil
- 1 large carrot
- 3 cloves garlic
- 1 medium green pepper
- 1 small onion

Method:

1. In a medium saucepan, heat the oil over moderate flame.

2. Combine the onion, tomato, and carrot in a mixing bowl.
3. Cook for an additional minute or until the veggies have softened.
4. Cook for thirty seconds after adding the garlic.
5. Mix in the chopped tomatoes, then insert the tomatoes, stock, corn, peas, smoked paprika, chili powder, and salt to taste.
6. Toss the rice with a fork to fluff it up.
7. After tasting, add the coriander and serve.

3.2 Tofu and Olive Tapas

Cooking Time: 43 minutes
Serving Size: 4

Ingredients:

For the Marinade

- ½ teaspoon black pepper
- ½ teaspoon chili flakes
- ½ teaspoon dried oregano
- ½ teaspoon salt
- 2 teaspoon paprika

For the Dish

- 50g Kalamata olives
- Small bunch of parsley
- 3 tablespoon vegetable stock
- 4 large plum tomatoes
- 4 tablespoon olive oil

- 1-star anise
- 3 tablespoon sherry
- ½ teaspoon chili flakes
- 3 cloves of garlic

Method:
1. Combine all of the components in a bowl or bag and stir well to combine the marinade.
2. Toss in the tofu and mix well. Cover and set aside for thirty minutes to marinate.
3. Cook the tofu parts in 2 tablespoons olive oil for 3-4 minutes, then set aside to keep warm.
4. In the cooking liquid, softly fry the garlic for 1-2 minutes.
5. Combine the chili flakes, chipotle powder, red wine, and vegetable stock in a large mixing bowl.
6. Cook, occasionally stirring, until the fluid has been reduced by half.
7. Medium heat for 2-3 minutes after adding the tofu, peppers, olives, and tarragon.
8. Serve with toasted bread right away.

3.3 Patatas Bravas

Cooking Time: 50 minutes

Serving Size: 12

Ingredients:

For the Sauce

- Pinch sugar
- Fresh parsley
- 2 teaspoon sweet paprika

- Good pinch chili powder
- 3 tablespoon olive oil
- 227g can tomatoes
- 1 tablespoon tomato purée
- 2 garlic cloves
- 1 small onion

For the Potatoes

- 2 tablespoon olive oil
- 900g potatoes

Method:

1. In a bowl, add the oil and cook the onions for about five minutes or until hardened.
2. Bring to the boil, stirring regularly, with the garlic, diced tomatoes, vegetable purée, adobo seasoning, chili powder, cinnamon, and salt pinch.
3. Heat for ten minutes, or until the mixture is pulpy.
4. Preheat the oven to 200 degrees Celsius.
5. Fry for 40-50 minutes until it's golden brown.
6. Spoon the pasta sauce over the vegetables in spice jars.
7. To eat, garnish with grated parmesan.

3.4 Mediterranean Seafood Stew

Cooking Time: 45 minutes
Serving Size: 6

Ingredients:
- 3 tablespoon toasted pine nuts
- Crusty Italian bread
- 2 lb. skinless sea bass fillet
- ½ cup fresh parsley leaves
- Olive oil
- ¼ cup golden raisins
- 2 tablespoon capers
- 1 large yellow onion
- 1 28-oz. can plum tomatoes
- 3 cups vegetable broth
- Pinch red pepper flakes
- ¾ cup dry white wine
- 2 celery ribs
- 4 large garlic cloves
- ½ teaspoon dried thyme
- Salt and pepper

Method:
1. 1 tablespoon olive oil, heated over moderate flame.
2. Add the onions, fennel, and a pinch of salt and pepper to taste.
3. Cook for a few minutes until the thyme, red pepper flakes, and cloves are aromatic.

4. Decrease the fluid by about ½ percent by getting it to a simmer.
5. Combine the peppers, vegetable broth, pecans, and chives in a large mixing bowl.
6. Cook for 15-20 minutes over a moderate flame, stirring periodically until the flavors have melded.
7. Place the fish parts in the liquid ingredients and gently stir them all together. Cover the Dutch oven and turn off the heat.
8. Mix in the chopped parsley last.
9. Fill serving bowls halfway with the spicy fish stew.

3.5 Spanish Orange & Olive Salad

Cooking Time: 20 minutes
Serving Size: 4

Ingredients:

For the Softened Leeks

- ¼ teaspoon kosher salt
- 1 tablespoon water
- 1 tablespoon white wine vinegar
- 1 small leek

For the Orange & Olive Salad

- Squeeze lemon juice
- ¼ cup Marcona almonds
- Sprinkle flaky sea salt
- Sprinkle Sumac
- 6 oranges
- 4 teaspoon leek vinegar marinade

- 1 tablespoon olive oil
- 3 tablespoon softened leeks
- ⅓ cup halved olives

Method:
1. To begin, prepare and marinate the leeks.
2. Cut the white color green pieces into rounds with a thin knife.
3. 1 tablespoon balsamic vinegar syrup, sea salt, and 1 tablespoon water are combined with the leeks.
4. Allow fifteen minutes for the leeks to caramelize, tossing periodically.
5. Cut the oranges into circles after segmenting them.
6. Cast aside half of the olives.
7. In a medium mixing bowl, combine the bananas, olives, and 3 tablespoons of the brined leeks.
8. Toss in 4 teaspoons of the leek marinade and 4 teaspoons of olive oil in a mixing bowl softly.
9. Add a pinch of flaky sea salt, sumac, a splash of lime juice, and nuts to the salad.
10. Serve directly after garnishing.

3.6 Mediterranean-Style Steamed Clams Recipe

Cooking Time: 1 hour

Serving Size: 4

Ingredients:

- 1 green onion
- ⅓ cup parsley
- 1 ½ cup water
- 3 pounds littleneck clams
- Extra virgin olive oil
- ½ teaspoon red pepper flakes
- 1 cup dry white wine
- 1 yellow onion
- ½ teaspoon cumin
- ½ teaspoon smoked paprika
- ½ green pepper
- Salt and pepper
- 2 ripe tomatoes
- 4 garlic cloves minced
- ½ red pepper

Method:

1. Clean the clams.
2. Put down the clams in the first container of cool simmering water for about 20 minutes.
3. To make the red wine soup, add all of the ingredients to a big mixing bowl.

4. ¼ cup olive oil, heated in a big Dutch oven over moderate flame.
5. Combine the onions, tomatoes, and garlic in a large mixing bowl.
6. Cook for five minutes after seasoning with kosher salt and black pepper.
7. Add the onions, smoked paprika, parmesan, and garlic powder, and stir to combine.
8. Combine the white wine and liquid in a mixing bowl.
9. Process for a few minutes, just until the tomato is slightly softened.
10. In a red wine sauce, heat the clams.
11. Reduce the heat to medium-low and add the clams.
12. Cook, covered until the remainder of the clams has opened.
13. Switch off the heat. Combine the spring onions and parsley in a mixing bowl.

3.7 Avocado and Tuna Tapas

Cooking Time: 20 minutes

Serving Size: 4

Ingredients:
- 1 pinch garlic salt
- 2 ripe avocados
- 1 dash balsamic vinegar
- Black pepper to taste
- 3 green onions

- ½ red bell pepper
- 1 tablespoon mayonnaise
- 1 can solid white tuna

Method:
1. In a mixing bowl, combine the tuna, mayo, spring onions, bell pepper, and maple syrup.
2. Dress with peppers and garlic salt, then stuff the tuna combination into the avocado halves.
3. Before eating, garnish with the reserved spring onions and a pinch of smoked paprika.

3.8 Fish Tapas

Cooking Time: 40 minutes

Serving Size: 4

Ingredients:
- 40g butter
- 500ml salt
- 110g peas
- 40g flour
- 1 carrot
- 1 bay leaf
- 200g flour
- 12 mussels
- 1 onion
- 100ml olive oil
- Salt
- 200g cod

- 3 tablespoons water
- 1 egg

Method:
1. Combine the flour, oil, yolk, liquid, and a bit of salt to make a pastry.
2. In boiled water, cook fish and mussels with cabbage, carrot, and lemon zest.
3. Strip the mussels from their skins until cooked and cut finely.
4. Remove some bones from the fish and chop it up.
5. In boiled water, prepare the vegetable peas.
6. Create a thick white liquid with the oil in a frying pan.
7. Combine the diced fish, mussels, and peas in a large mixing bowl.
8. Seal the sides of the pastry by folding it over.
9. Keep 10 to 15 minutes in a deep fryer.
10. Serve with fried tarragon on the side.

3.9 Garlic Soup with Egg and Croutons

Cooking Time: 35 minutes

Serving Size: 2

Ingredients:
- ¼ cup extra virgin olive oil
- Salt and pepper
- 1 teaspoon sweet paprika
- 1-liter chicken broth

- 2 eggs
- 6 garlic cloves
- 2 slices of stale bread

Method:
1. Peel the garlic and cut into strips.
2. Heat the olive oil in a saucepan over medium heat.
3. Add garlic and cook for 2-3 minutes, or until it starts to brown.
4. Add the loaf to the pan and fry it with the garlic, allowing it to soak up the oil.
5. Reduce to low heat and stir in the parmesan.
6. Put in the liquid and give it a good swirl.
7. Take the soup to a rolling simmer, reduce to low heat, and continue cooking for about thirty minutes.
8. To taste, season with salt and pepper, using at least ½ teaspoon pepper.
9. In a large mixing bowl, whisk together the eggs and add them to the soup.

3.10 Spanish Tapas-Style Green Pepper

Cooking Time: 5 minutes

Serving Size: 2

Ingredients:
- 2 tablespoon olive oil
- Pinch of sea salt flakes
- 250g green peppers

Method:

1. Wipe down the peppers in ice water.
2. In a big nonstick roasting tray, heat the oil.
3. Cook the peppers for 4-5 minutes, or till their surfaces peel and become brown.
4. To drain, place them on some paper towels.
5. Serve promptly with a pinch of sea salt.

3.11 Magdalenas: Spanish Lemon Cupcakes

Cooking Time: 1 hour
Serving Size: 10

Ingredients:

- 1 tablespoon baking powder
- Pinch salt
- 1 teaspoon vanilla extract
- 1 1/3 cups pastry flour
- 3 large eggs
- ¼ cup milk
- Zest from 1 lemon
- ½ cup extra virgin olive oil
- ½ cup granulated sugar

Method:

1. Add the eggs to a big mixing bowl until bright and powdery.
2. Slowly incorporate the sugar, then the olive oil and milk.
3. Combine the lemon zest and vanilla essence in a mixing bowl.

4. Mix in the flour, icing sugar, and salt until there are no chunks.
5. Put it in the fridge for thirty minutes after covering the dish.
6. Preheat the oven to 425 degrees Fahrenheit.
7. Use two-thirds of the batter in each muffin container, and sugar can be sprinkled on top if needed.
8. Decrease the heat to 400 degrees Fahrenheit and position it in the oven.
9. Cook the Magdalenas for 13-fifteen minutes, or until raised and translucent from around edges.
10. Warm or at ambient temperature is perfect.

3.12 Cucumber Tapas

Cooking Time: 30 minutes

Serving Size: 4

Ingredients:
- Pinch of black pepper
- 1 tablespoon oregano
- 2 ounces feta cheese
- ¼ teaspoon salt
- 2 tablespoons olive oil
- 1 teaspoon sherry vinegar
- 2 cucumbers

Method:
1. Remove the seeds from cucumbers by slicing them lengthwise.

2. Dice cucumber into ¼-inch pieces and place in a small cup.
3. Toss in the canola oil, mustard, feta cheese, pepper, and spice to mix. Toss in the oregano and toss once more.
4. Remove 1 or 2 thin pieces of peel from underneath each cucumber half with a potato peeler, so they don't tip over.
5. Distribute the cucumber-and-feta combination between them.
6. Cut cucumbers into 1 ½-inch piece on a slight triangular and serve right away.

Chapter 4: Tapas Lunch and Dinner Recipes

4.1 Spanish Style Rice

Cooking Time: 45 minutes
Serving Size: 8
Ingredients:
- ½ teaspoon salt
- Chopped cilantro for garnish
- 2 teaspoons cumin
- 1 teaspoon chili powder
- ¾ cup corn kernels
- ½ cup frozen peas
- 1 cup tomatoes
- 2 2/3 cups vegetable broth
- 1½ cups white rice
- 1 tablespoon tomato paste
- 3 tablespoons olive oil
- 1 large carrot
- 3 cloves garlic
- 1 medium green pepper
- 1 small onion

Method:
1. In a medium saucepan, heat the oil over moderate flame.

2. Combine the onion, tomato, and carrot in a mixing bowl.
3. Cook for an additional minute or until the veggies have softened.
4. Cook for thirty seconds after adding the garlic.
5. Mix in the chopped tomatoes, then insert the tomatoes, stock, corn, peas, smoked paprika, chili powder, and salt to taste.
6. Toss the rice with a fork to fluff it up.
7. After tasting, add the coriander and serve.

4.2 Mediterranean Basa Stew & Sunny Aioli

Cooking Time: 1 hour

Serving Size: 2

Ingredients:
- 1 white wine vinegar
- 1 carrot
- 1 garlic clove
- 1 tomato paste
- 2 ciabatta rolls
- 1 mayonnaise
- 1 garlic clove
- 1 vegetable stock
- 1 brown onion
- 1 teaspoon ground turmeric
- 5g parsley
- 2 x 100g basa fillets

- 1-star anise
- 1 bag of pitted black olives

Method:

1. Preheat the oven to 220 degrees Celsius.
2. Use a drizzle of canola oil, heat a big, wide-based pan.
3. Insert the chopped onion, sliced carrot, and a quarter of the garlic once the pan is warmed.
4. Heat for 6-8 minutes, just until the onions are soft and transparent, after adding the star anise.
5. Whisk together the mayo, the leftover minced garlic, the red wine vinegar, and add salt and pepper.
6. Place the ciabatta rolls on a baking sheet and bake them for 8-10 minutes.
7. Warm a drizzle of olive oil in a separate wide broad pan over medium temperature.
8. When the pan is warmed, skin-side up, add the sea bass, and boil for four minutes.
9. With the warm ciabatta on the side, place the grilled sea bass over the soup.

4.3 25-Minute Shrimp and Chorizo

Cooking Time: 25 minutes

Serving Size: 6

Ingredients:
- Boiling water
- 1 cup fresh parsley
- 1.5 lb. large shrimp
- 1 ¼ cup couscous
- 1 ¼ teaspoon ground cumin
- Salt
- 1 ¼ teaspoon turmeric
- 1 ¼ teaspoon paprika
- 6 oz. hard Spanish Chorizo
- 3 garlic cloves
- 2 jalapeno peppers
- 1 small yellow onion
- Extra virgin olive

Method:
1. Heat a small amount of vegetable oil in a large frying pan.
2. Heat the Chorizo sausage rolls until they are crisp.
3. Remove from the heat and clean on towels.
4. Add the garlic, onions, and habanero to the boiling pot and cook till the vegetables are transparent.

5. Now insert the seasoning and mix for a few seconds before adding the shrimp.
6. Heat the shrimp for approximately 3 minutes on moderate flame.
7. In the meantime, bring 2 ½ cups of water to a boil.
8. Transfer the couscous, little more vegetable oil, a pinch of salt, and the hot oil to the frying pan with the Chorizo.
9. Allow for five minutes of resting time. Remove the cover and add the fresh parsley.
10. Enjoy by moving to serve pots.

4.4 Spanish Rice Dinner

Cooking Time: 20 minutes

Serving Size: 4

Ingredients:

- ⅛ teaspoon pepper
- ⅛ teaspoon hot pepper sauce
- ½ teaspoon ground mustard
- ¼ teaspoon garlic powder
- 1 teaspoon salt
- 1 teaspoon Worcestershire sauce
- 1 tablespoon onion
- 1 tablespoon sugar
- 1 can stewed tomatoes
- 1 can green beans
- 1-½ cups cooked rice

- 1 pound ground beef

Method:

1. Steam beef when no pinker in a large frying pan; clean.
2. Add the rest of the ingredients and stir to combine.
3. Raise the temperature to be high and bring the mixture to a boil.
4. Reduce to a low heat environment, cover, and cook for 5-10 minutes, or until thoroughly cooked.

4.5 Spicy Crab Salad Tapas

Cooking Time: 35 minutes

Serving Size: 10

Ingredients:

- 1 large egg
- 1 tablespoon water
- ¼ teaspoon pepper
- 1 package pastry
- 1 can lump crabmeat
- ½ cup mayonnaise
- ½ teaspoon salt
- ¼ cup sweet red pepper
- 2 garlic cloves
- 1 teaspoon mustard
- ¼ cup sweet yellow pepper
- 1 tablespoon cilantro

- 1 tablespoon lemon juice
- 1 jalapeno pepper
- ¼ cup green onions

Method:
1. Preheat the oven to 375 degrees Fahrenheit.
2. Mix the first twelve ingredients in a mixing bowl.
3. Refrigerate for at least 1 hour, sealed.
4. In the meantime, roll out puff pastry on a lightly floured.
5. Roll pastry into a 10-inch square and cut into twenty-five 2-inch squares.
6. Brush pastry with a mixture of egg and water.
7. Position cutout pieces on top of strong squares and move to baking sheets lined with parchment paper.
8. Bake for eighteen minutes, or until lightly browned.
9. Bring to room temperature before serving.
10. Place 1 heaping tablespoon of smoked salmon in the center of each cooked pastry once it has cooled.

4.6 Pulpo Gallego: A Galician-Style Octopus Tapas

Cooking Time: 40 minutes

Serving Size: 4

Ingredients:
- Spanish smoked paprika
- Extra virgin olive oil
- 500g of potatoes
- Sea salt flakes
- 1 whole octopus

Method:
1. Once the water starts to boil, bring a big pot of water on the stove with a grain of salt.
2. On medium-high heat, roast your octopus for 15 to 20 minutes.
3. Ensure that the octopus remains submerged in water during the cooking process.
4. Octopus, like spaghetti, must be al dente.
5. Enable the octopus to rest throughout the liquid ingredients for a few minutes after it has finished cooking.
6. Break the octopus tentacles and vegetables into ½ inch thick slices to eat.
7. Table salt, cayenne pepper, and a healthy drizzle of olive oil complete the dish.

4.7 Roasted Vegetable Tapas

Cooking Time: 35 minutes

Serving Size: 8

Ingredients:
- Small handful parsley
- ½ teaspoon paprika
- Zest 0.5 lemon
- 8 basil leaves
- 1 large aubergine
- 25g parmesan
- 3 sundried tomatoes
- 1 large courgette
- 3 tablespoon olive oil
- 250g tub ricotta
- 1 garlic clove
- 2 flame-roasted peppers

Method:
1. Slice the aubergine and courgette onto small, 2-3mm-thick slices.
2. Preheat a griddle pan to medium-high heat.
3. Pour the garlic oil on the vegetable strips and roast for 2-3 minutes on each side until it's soft and finely charred.
4. Combine the cheeses, sundried tomato, lime juice, and spice in a mixing bowl.

5. Arrange the aubergine strips on a big cutting board.
6. A strip of courgette, a slice of spice, and basil leaves go on top of each.
7. Organize on a plate and top with parsley leaf and paprika when ready to eat.

4.8 Chicken Tapas with Romesco Sauce

Cooking Time: 50 minutes

Serving Size: 4

Ingredients:

- 2 garlic cloves
- Sea salt and pepper
- 2 tablespoon extra-virgin olive oil
- 3 sprigs of thyme
- 12 chicken thighs

For the Romesco Sauce

- ½ teaspoon of smoked paprika
- Salt and pepper to taste
- 1 tablespoon sherry vinegar
- ½ teaspoon of cumin seeds
- 2 whole red peppers
- 12 whole hazelnuts, skin off
- 6 tablespoon olive oil
- 2 ripe tomatoes
- 1 garlic clove
- 12 Marcona almonds

- 1 piece of stale bread

Method:
1. Preheat the grill on your stove.
2. Position the peppers halves on a plate, skin cut side.
3. Take the steaks from the barbecue and cover them with a kitchen towel. Cut the peppers into large pieces.
4. To create the romesco salsa, gently toast the star anise in a small deep fryer to expel their oil.
5. Transfer the diced veggies, peppers, bread, cloves, almonds, walnuts, smoked paprika, cayenne pepper, balsamic vinegar, and sherry vinegar to a food processor till a crunchy paste with the texture of pesto forms.
6. Heat the oven to 200°C for the chicken breasts.
7. Sprinkle the olive oil over the chicken breasts on a sheet and sprinkle with salt.
8. Cook the chicken breasts for 3 minutes on each side in a warm deep fryer.
9. Roast for thirty minutes cut side down, with the tarragon and garlic.
10. Offer the marinated chicken thighs with romesco sauces, smashed almonds, and a squeeze of lemon juice on a base of romesco marinade.

4.9 Fried Chorizo with Chick Peas and Tomatoes

Cooking Time: 20 minutes

Serving Size: 4

Ingredients:
- Salt and pepper
- 3 tablespoons parsley
- 2 pints cherry tomatoes
- 1 teaspoon smoked paprika
- 9 ounces chorizo
- 2 15-oz. cans chickpeas
- 1 onion
- 1 tablespoon olive oil

Method:
1. In a saucepan over medium heat, steam the oil.
2. Sauté onion for three minutes, or until soft.
3. Toss in the chorizo.
4. Sauté for 30 seconds to 1 minute, or until thoroughly hot.
5. Combine chickpeas, grape tomatoes, and paprika in a mixing bowl.
6. Cook for 8 minutes, or until tomatoes are softened and liquids are boiling.
7. Salt and pepper to taste. Serve with a tarragon garnish.

4.10 Boquerones Al Limon

Cooking Time: 30 minutes
Serving Size: 2

Ingredients:
- Chickpea flour
- Salt
- 1 clove of garlic
- 1 bunch of parsley
- 1 lemon
- 350 grams anchovies

Method:
1. Clean and dry the anchovies.
2. Place the garlic, tarragon, and pepper in a mortar and use the pestle to grind them into a powder.
3. Combine the paste with the extract of one lemon.
4. Place the fillets in a crystal tray and spill the marinade over them.
5. Cover the plate with plastic wrap and refrigerate for up to two hours to soak.
6. Take off the extra chickpea flour after passing them through.
7. In a large pan, heat some butter over medium heat.
8. Fry 4-5 at the moment for 1 minute, or till they transform a lovely golden color.
9. To absorb excess oil, place the fried fish on a plate lined with towels.
10. Serve with lime wedges and aioli sauce.

4.11 Spanish Tapas Platter

Cooking Time: 1 hour 15 minutes

Serving Size: 8

Ingredients:
- 2 cups green grapes
- 1 crusty loaf of bread
- 1 cup redskin Spanish peanuts
- 8 ounces fig spread
- 3.75 ounce can of sardines
- 4 ounces cheddar
- 1 cup Spanish olives pitted
- 3 ounces salami
- 4 ounces manchego
- 4 ounces prosciutto
- 4 ounces tavern ham
- 3 ounces sausage
- 3 ounces serrano ham

Method:
1. In separate bowls, position the olives, almonds, and fig scatter.
2. In a serving dish or shallow cup, position the sardines.
3. Organize the sardines on the large plate, along with the bowls of artichokes, nuts, and figs. Allow plenty of space between them.

4. After this, on the large plate, organize the meat and the Iberico cheese to fill most of the large area.
5. Grape bunches, cheese crackers, and sandwich slices may be used to fill up the gaps.
6. To make it easier to reach the objects, keep them close but not too near together.
7. Place the leftover bread in a bucket near the stove.

4.12 Catalan Fig Tapas

Cooking Time: 15 minutes

Serving Size: 4

Ingredients:

- 4 slices Jamon
- 100g manchego cheese
- 8 slices of wood-fired bread
- 1 garlic clove
- 8 figs
- 6 thyme sprigs
- ¼ cup olive oil

Method:

1. Preheat a chargrill or a barbecue to high temperature.
2. Toss the doubled figs with canola oil, minced parsley, and a bit of salt in a mixing cup.
3. Roast the figs for two minutes on each hand or until they are soft and caramelized.

4. Rub the bread with excess oil in both directions and grill for 1-two minutes on either side until it's crispy and charred.
5. Place two fig pieces on each chargrilled loaf piece.
6. Serve hot, topped with Jamun and grilled manchego.

4.13 Quick and Easy Paella

Cooking Time: 1 hour 10 minutes

Serving Size: 6

Ingredients:

Saffron Broth

- ½ teaspoon saffron threads
- 2 ¼ cups chicken broth
- 2 teaspoons olive oil
- 1 pound jumbo shrimp

Paella

- 1 teaspoon paprika
- 1 pinch cayenne pepper
- 1 red bell pepper
- Salt to taste
- 1 ⅓ cups Arborio rice
- ½ cup green peas
- 1 tablespoon olive oil
- ½ yellow onion
- 2 cloves garlic

- 8 ounces chorizo sausage

Method:

1. In a pan over medium heat, steam, and mix preserved shrimp shells and two teaspoons canola oil.
2. Stir saffron into the shells, and add the chicken broth.
3. Preheat the oven to 425 degrees Fahrenheit.
4. In a large oven-safe skillet, heat one tablespoon of olive oil on medium-high heat. In a hot skillet, cook chorizo strips.
5. Continue cooking the garlic into the chorizo combination until moist.
6. Over the rice, place the seafood in a thin layer.
7. Sprinkle with salt, parmesan, and cayenne pepper, and place pepper slices around as well as between shrimp.
8. Cook the rice paste for 20 minutes in a preheated oven.
9. Cook, often stirring, until the rice is soft, the liquid has been absorbed, and the rice has caramelized.

4.14 Tapas & Pinchos Vegetarian

Cooking Time: 30 minutes

Serving Size: 2

Ingredients:

Garlic Aioli Ingredients

- ½ cup olive oil
- Salt to taste

- 1 teaspoon lemon juice
- 1 egg yolk
- 1 garlic clove

Tomato Sauce Ingredients
- 2 teaspoons smoked paprika
- Salt and pepper to taste
- 1 garlic clove
- 1 red jalapeno
- 1 tablespoon olive oil
- 3 large plum tomatoes

Potato Ingredients
- 2 tablespoons olive oil
- Salt and pepper to taste
- 1 lb. potatoes

Garnish Ingredients
- Fresh lemon juice
- 1 tablespoon parsley

Method:
1. Preheat the oven to 400 degrees Fahrenheit.
2. Toss potato in canola oil and season with salt and pepper.
3. Position on a cookie sheet in a single sheet.
4. Cook for 25 to 30 minutes until its fork ready.
5. In a spice grinder, puree the vegetables to make the sauce.
6. Add the oil to a pan.
7. Add garlic and jalapeno peppers at this stage.

8. Insert pureed onions, cayenne pepper, salt, and pepper until the onions have softened.
9. Combine the garlic, lime juice, and egg white in a mixing dish.
10. Beat the egg yolks with an immersion blender until they are light in color.
11. Continue to beat until it thickens into a sour cream texture.
12. Mix in the salt until it is well combined.
13. Put potatoes in a dish to eat.

Chapter 5: Vegetarian Tapas Recipes

5.1 Spanish Vegan Paella

Cooking Time: 45 minutes

Serving Size: 5

Ingredients:

- 2 sprigs of fresh thyme
- ¾ cup frozen peas
- 1 teaspoon sea salt
- Fresh cracked pepper
- 3 tablespoons olive oil
- 1 teaspoon smoked paprika
- ½ teaspoon sweet paprika
- 4 cups vegetable broth
- 1 large tomato
- 1 ½ cups Bomba Rice
- 1 red bell pepper
- 5 cloves garlic
- 1 medium onion
- 1 teaspoon saffron threads

Method:

1. In a small saucepan, insert vegetable broth.
2. In a 12-inch Paella Bowl, heat two tablespoons of oil and add the vegetables and spices.
3. Sauté until the vegetables are tender and golden brown.

4. Sauté for two minutes after adding the garlic.
5. Combine the onions, spicy paprika, and sweet paprika in a mixing bowl.
6. Cook for 1-2 minutes on high heat.
7. In the same pan, add the rice and the leftover 1 tablespoon of oil.
8. Put in the liquid slowly while adding the fresh thyme. Season with salt and pepper.
9. Reduce the heat to a low simmer.
10. Switch off the heat in the pan. Toss in the peas on top of the rice.

5.2 Smoked Vegetarian Spanish Rice Recipe

Cooking Time: 45 minutes

Serving Size: 4

Ingredients:

- 1 coal
- Salt, to taste
- ½ teaspoon red chili powder
- ¼ cheddar cheese
- 1 cups basmati rice
- ¼ cup sweet corn
- ¼ cup green peas
- 2 tablespoons olive oil
- 3 tomatoes
- 2 stalks celery
- 1 onion

- 4 cloves garlic
- 1 green bell pepper
- 2 green chilies

Method:

1. In a large skillet, heat the oil over moderate heat and cook the garlic, onion, green pepper, diced peppers, and fennel until ready.
2. On low to moderate heat, sauté the vegetables and bell peppers until they are fully soft.
3. Add the onion, pepper, and chili powder once they have softened, and continue to cook until the vegetables are soft and tender.
4. Add the rice, beans, carrots, salt, and peppers, as well as two cups of water to the pot.
5. Turn the heat down and let the Spanish rice sit for around ten minutes after cooking.
6. Pour a teaspoon of ghee or oil over the hot coal.
7. The rice will absorb the flavors of the smoked meat.
8. To mix all of the flavors and ingredients in the Spinach Rice, stir it thoroughly.

5.3 Champinones Spanish Garlic Mushrooms

Cooking Time: 10 minutes

Serving Size: 4

Ingredients:

- ½ teaspoon chili flakes
- 1 tablespoon flat-leaf parsley
- ¼ teaspoon Spanish paprika

- Ground pepper and sea salt
- 10 large button mushrooms
- 1 tablespoon lemon juice
- 2 tablespoons dry sherry
- 3 tablespoons olive oil
- 5 cloves garlic

Method:

1. Quarter the mushrooms, chop the parsley, and crush the garlic.
2. Add the olive oil and simmer the mushrooms for several moments over moderate flame.
3. Then, with the exception of the parsley, combine the rest of the ingredients.
4. Cook for another five minutes, stirring occasionally.
5. Then take the pan from the heat and whisk in the grated parmesan.

5.4 Spanish Vegetarian Tapas

Cooking Time: 20 minutes

Serving Size: 4

Ingredients:

- 1 tablespoon olive oil
- Fresh basil
- 1 red onion
- 1 dl mató cheese
- 1 bag of dates
- 250g small tomatoes

- 2 clove of garlic
- 2 tablespoon mató cheese
- A handful walnuts
- 1 eggplant
- 1 tablespoon maple syrup

Method:
1. Roll the dates and fill them with hazelnuts and Spanish Mató cheese.
2. Place on a tray and drizzle with maple syrup to finish.
3. Wash the tomatoes and cut them in half.
4. Chop parsley and red onion.
5. Combine the tomato and Mató cheese in a mixing dish.
6. Wash the eggplant and break it into thinly sliced.
7. Grill for 2-3 minutes on each side after brushing with canola oil.
8. Cover them in foil and place them on a tray.
9. Place olive tapenade, polenta, cello, oranges, artichokes, manchego cheese, heat tomatoes, fluffy biscuits, and Spanish wine on the tapas table.

5.5 Spanish Vegetarian Stew

Cooking Time: 1 hour 20 minutes

Serving Size: 8

Ingredients:
- 1 teaspoon honey
- 2 small zucchini
- 1.5 cans tomatoes passata
- 1.5 teaspoons salt
- 1 green bell pepper
- 2 garlic cloves
- 1 large eggplant
- ½ long red chili
- 1 red bell pepper
- Good quality olive oil
- 1 large onion
- ½ teaspoon salt

Method:
1. Spray the eggplant with salts and slice it into pieces.
2. In a large frying pan, pour 4 tablespoons of vegetable oil.
3. Combine the onions, chili, and sliced peppers in a large mixing bowl.
4. Cook for ten minutes after adding the cloves and tomato.
5. Heat for 4-5 minutes, just until the eggplant is slightly golden brown.

6. Take the eggplant from the pan and drizzle with a little more coconut oil.
7. Heat, mixing a couple of times, for another 4-5 minutes with the zucchini.
8. Ultimately, mix in the pre-fried eggplant and sweet potato to the tomato mixture in the cup.
9. After frying, set aside for five minutes before serving.

5.6 Spanish Tapas-Inspired Mussels

Cooking Time: 40 minutes

Serving Size: 2

Ingredients:

- ¼ cup dry sherry
- 2 pounds mussels
- Pinch of saffron
- ½ cup vegetable broth
- 2 teaspoons olive oil
- 2 teaspoons fresh oregano
- ½ teaspoon pepper
- 1 8-ounce can chickpeas
- 2 cloves garlic
- 1 4-ounce jar pimientos
- 1 small onion
- 8 cherry tomatoes

Method:

1. In a medium skillet, heat the oil over moderate flame.

2. Combine the chickpeas, onions, ginger, garlic, and pimentos in a large mixing bowl.
3. Process until tender, five to six minutes, stirring constantly.
4. Add oregano, cinnamon, and saffron and stir to combine.
5. Cook for about thirty seconds, stirring constantly.
6. Stir in the broth and red wine, scraping up any browned bits from the bottom of the pan.
7. Bring the liquid to a low boil, then reduce to low heat.
8. Stir in the mussels. Reduce the heat to a low temperature and keep it there.
9. Cover, lower heat, and cook for five to six minutes, or until mussels open.
10. When serving, stir in the mussels and remove any that haven't opened.

5.7 Tapas Style Garlic Mushrooms

Cooking Time: 10 minutes

Serving Size: 4

Ingredients:

- 1 tablespoon lemon juice
- 2 tablespoons fresh parsley
- Salt to taste
- ½ cup white wine
- 4 garlic cloves
- 2 pounds mushrooms
- 2 tablespoons olive oil

Method:
1. In a large skillet over medium heat, add the oil over moderate flame.
2. Cook the mushroom for five minutes, periodically tossing the pot.
3. Heat, flipping the pan often, for another 1-2 minutes or until crispy, adding the garlic, cayenne pepper, salt, and pepper.
4. Toss in the tarragon to mix everything.
5. Serve with aioli and lime wedges alongside the mushrooms.

5.8 Spanish Rice Skillet Meal

Cooking Time: 28 minutes

Serving Size: 4

Ingredients:

- 1 can tomatoes
- 1 can tomatoes with green chilies
- ⅛ teaspoon black pepper
- ½ cup water
- ½ teaspoon cumin
- ¼ teaspoon salt
- ¾ pound ground beef
- ¼ teaspoon oregano
- ½ teaspoon chili powder
- 2 tablespoons olive oil
- 1 clove garlic
- ¾ cup uncooked white rice

- ½ medium onion

Method:

1. In a large frying pan, brown the ground beef, stirring constantly.
2. Drain the water and set it aside.
3. On moderate flame, drizzle vegetable oil into the pan.
4. Sauté onions for three minutes, or until soft.
5. Mix in the garlic and grain until the rice is finely browned.
6. Combine the ground beef, oregano, chili powder, smoked paprika, salt, black pepper, and tomatoes in a large mixing bowl.
7. Get the water to a boil.
8. Reduce to medium heat, cover, and cook for 20 minutes, or till all liquid has been absorbed.

5.9 Mediterranean Baked Tapas

Cooking Time: 15 minutes

Serving Size: 4

Ingredients:

- 3 tablespoon olive oil
- 110g sundried tomatoes
- 8 cloves garlic
- 110g chorizo sausages

Method:

1. Set the oven to 150 degrees Celsius.

2. Heat a whole clove, chorizo treats, and quasi tomato in a tiny cast-iron skillet with just a little canola oil for 2-three minutes on the hot plate.
3. Place the whole combination in the oven and continue to cook for 10-12 minutes.
4. Turn off the heat and set aside to cool moderately before brushing with the residual oil and serve with toasted bread.

5.10 Chorizo and Potato Tapas

Cooking Time: 40 minutes

Serving Size: 6

Ingredients:

- 1kg new potatoes
- 250g small cooking chorizo
- Pinch smoked paprika
- 400g can tomato
- 1 tablespoon olive oil
- 1 red chili
- Pinch cayenne pepper
- 2 garlic cloves
- 1 onion

Method:

1. In a bowl, heat a little more oil and cook the onions, garlic, and chili till the onion loosens, then mix in the smoked paprika and parmesan.

2. Bring the tomatoes to a low boil, then reduce to low heat. Season to taste and blend with a stand mixer.
3. In the meantime, steam the potato for ten minutes when slowly cooking the chorizo and releasing some of its oil in a deep fryer.
4. Remove any excess red oil and replace it with 1 tablespoon olive oil.
5. Fry all together, including the potatoes. Pour into a mixing dish.

Chapter 6: Classic Spanish Dishes

6.1 Mediterranean Skillet Chicken with Bulgur Paella, Carrots

Cooking Time: 50 minutes

Serving Size: 4

Ingredients:

Lemon Yogurt Sauce

- Pinch of cayenne pepper
- Kosher salt
- Zest and juice of 1 lemon
- 2 tablespoons curly parsley
- 1½ cups plain yogurt

For the Chicken

- ½ cup golden raisins
- ½ cup curly parsley sprigs
- 2 cups safflower oil
- ½ cup whole blanched almonds
- 6 chicken thighs
- 2 bay leaves
- 1½ cups basmati rice
- 4 whole cloves
- 2 cinnamon sticks
- 3 cups chicken stock
- 5 cardamom pods

- 6 chicken drumsticks
- 2 tablespoons tomato paste
- 3 strips orange zest
- Kosher salt and pepper
- ½ teaspoon turmeric
- 2 tomatoes
- 2 tablespoons olive oil
- 1 teaspoon cumin
- 1 teaspoon coriander
- 1 large onion
- 2 teaspoons fresh ginger
- ½ cup grated carrot
- 3 cloves garlic

Method:
1. Combine yogurt, lime juice and zest, tarragon, and smoked paprika in a medium mixing cup.
2. Put aside after seasoning with salt.
3. Preheat the oven to 375 degrees Fahrenheit.
4. Season the chicken with salt and pepper before serving.
5. Reduce the heat to medium-low and add the spices.
6. Place them skin-side up golden brown chicken in the boiling liquid and bake for 25 minutes.
7. Take the rice to a boil in a saucepan with the stored liquid ingredients over moderate flame.

8. Stir in the rice, cover, and cook on low heat until the rice is tender about 20 minutes.

6.2 One Pan Spanish Chicken and Rice Recipe with Chorizo

Cooking Time: 1 hour

Serving Size: 5

Ingredients:

For Chicken

- 3 tablespoon tomato paste
- 3 cups chicken broth
- 2 garlic cloves
- 1 large ripe tomato
- 1 ½ cup rice
- 1 large green bell pepper
- 1 medium red onion
- 4 chicken thighs
- Olive oil
- 6 oz. bulk chorizo sausage
- 4 chicken drumsticks

For Spice Rub

- 1 teaspoon black pepper
- ½ teaspoon cayenne pepper
- 1 teaspoon garlic powder
- 1 teaspoon salt
- 1 tablespoon smoked paprika

Method:
1. Soak the grain in water for a few minutes.
2. Position the rice in a bowl after thoroughly rinsing it.
3. Combine the ingredients, salt, and peppers in a small cup.
4. Dress the chicken with salt and pepper.
5. Brown both sides of the chicken.
6. Cautiously put the chicken in the pot and cook both sides thoroughly.
7. Transfer the chorizo to the same plate.
8. Combine the green beans, onions, and garlic in a large mixing bowl.
9. Cook for five minutes over a moderate flame, stirring frequently.
10. Combine the sliced tomatoes, tomato sauce, and chicken stock in a large mixing bowl.
11. Return the browned poultry to the bowl. Cook for 20 to 30 minutes at 350°F.
12. Cook the rice in the same pot as the chicken.
13. Allow the chicken and rice to rest in the pan for a few minutes.

6.3 Spanish Mixed Green Salad

Cooking Time: 10 minutes

Serving Size: 4

Ingredients:

- ½ Spanish onion
- 10 -12 green olives
- 2 cups Boston lettuce
- 2 tomatoes
- 1 cup baby spinach
- 2 cups romaine lettuce

Dressing

- 3 tablespoons olive oil
- Sea salt and black pepper
- 1 tablespoon lemon juice

Method:

1. Combine all of the dressing components in a mixing bowl and whisk until thoroughly combined.
2. Toss with salad well before eating.

6.4 Saucy Spanish Chicken with Green Olives

Cooking Time: 150 minutes

Serving Size: 8

Ingredients:
- ¼ cup sherry
- 1 tablespoon cornstarch
- 2 teaspoon dried thyme
- 1 teaspoon cumin and paprika
- 8 chicken drumsticks
- 1 small red onion
- 2 large garlic cloves
- 1 cup green olives
- 389ml can tomato sauce

Method:
1. Remove the skin from the chicken and remove any excess fat.
2. Pour the sauce in. Quantify out the artichokes, then cut them up and throw them in.
3. Combine the onion, ginger, thyme, smoked paprika, and tarragon in a mixing bowl.
4. Place the chicken in the paste to coat it, then turn it bone-side out. Push your way into the liquid.
5. Cook for six hours on medium or 2½ to 3 hours on average, or until chicken reaches 165°F.
6. Combine cornstarch and a few tablespoons of water in a mixing bowl and whisk until smooth.

7. Stir frequently in the sauce until it thickens, around five minutes. Serve chicken over rice.

6.5 Pisto

Cooking Time: 1 hour 20 minutes

Serving Size: 8

Ingredients:
- 1 teaspoon honey
- 2 medium zucchini
- 1.5 cans tomatoes
- 1.5 teaspoons salt
- 1 green bell pepper
- 2 garlic cloves
- 1 large eggplant
- ½ long red chili
- 1 red bell pepper
- Good quality olive oil
- 1 large onion
- ½ teaspoon salt

Method:
1. Spray the eggplant with salts and slice it into pieces.
2. Allow for 15-20 minutes of rest time.
3. In a big, roasting pan, heat four tablespoons of canola oil over moderate flame.
4. Combine the onions, chili, and diced beans in a large mixing bowl. Cook for 12-14 minutes over moderate flame.

5. Fry for 4-5 minutes, mixing halfway through, until the eggplant is golden brown.
6. Remove the eggplant from the pan and drizzle with a little more canola oil.
7. Cook for another 4-5 minutes after adding the zucchini.
8. Ultimately, mix in the pre-fried zucchini and eggplant to the tomatoes concentrate in the pot.
9. Cover and cook for 25 minutes over a moderate flame with a seal.

6.6 Easy Seafood Paella Recipe

Cooking Time: 1 hour

Serving Size: 6

Ingredients:

- 1 lb. prawns
- ¼ cup fresh parsley
- 2 large Roma tomatoes
- 6 oz. French green beans
- 4 small lobster tails
- ½ teaspoon chili pepper flakes
- Salt
- Water
- 1 teaspoon Spanish paprika
- 1 teaspoon cayenne pepper
- 3 tablespoon olive oil
- 4 garlic cloves
- 2 large pinches of saffron

- 2 cups Spanish rice
- 1 large yellow onion

Method:

1. Take 3 cups of water to a gentle simmer in a big saucepan.
2. Tongs are used to cut the lobster tails.
3. After 2 minutes of sautéing the onions, add the garlic and cook for another 3 minutes, stirring frequently.
4. Combine the saffron, dripping water, paprika, smoked paprika, Aleppo paprika, and salt in a mixing bowl.
5. Combine the tomato slices and green beans in a mixing bowl.
6. Cook for an additional ten minutes, just until the seafood changes color.
7. Add the cooked seafood chunks last.
8. Serve with rosemary as a garnish.
9. With your favorite white wine, eat the paella sweet.

6.7 Gambas al Ajillo

Cooking Time: 20 minutes

Serving Size: 4

Ingredients:

- 2 tablespoons dry sherry
- 1 tablespoon Italian parsley
- 1 teaspoon hot smoked paprika
- ¼ cup extra-virgin olive oil

- 1 pound shrimp
- 4 cloves garlic

Method:

1. Finely cut garlic. Paprika and sea salt are used to season the shrimp. To coat, mix it.
2. In a pan, cook the garlic and oil on moderate flame.
3. Cook for about two minutes or until the garlic begins to turn translucent.
4. Increase the heat to the extreme and add the shrimp.
5. Toss and rotate the shrimp with tongs for around two minutes or until they start to curl but are still uncooked.
6. Pour the sherry in. Heat, constantly stirring, for 1 minute more, or till sauces come to boiling and shrimp is fried through.
7. Remove the pan from the heat. With a spoon, fold in the parsley.

6.8 Easy Spanish Tortilla Recipe

Cooking Time: 50 minutes

Serving Size: 4

Ingredients:

- 8 eggs, beaten
- Handful flat-leaf parsley
- 400g waxy potatoes
- 6 garlic cloves
- 4 tablespoon olive oil

- 25g butter
- 1 large white onion

To Serve
- 4 vine tomatoes
- Drizzle of olive oil
- 1 baguette

Method:
1. Preheat a large nonstick deep fryer to medium.
2. Steadily roast the onion in the butter and oil until it is tender. Slice the tomatoes in the meantime.
3. Add the potatoes to the skillet, wrap, and cook for another 15-20 minutes, occasionally mixing to ensure even cooking.
4. Add 2 garlic cloves crushed and mixed in, followed by pounded eggs.
5. Replace the lid on the pan and bake the tortilla on low heat.
6. When the tortilla is finished, move it to a plate and eat it warm or hot, with grated parmesan on top.

6.9 Easy Spanish Garlic Soup

Cooking Time: 45 minutes

Serving Size: 4

Ingredients:
- ¼ cup flat-leaf parsley
- 4 large eggs
- 1 pinch cayenne pepper

- Salt and black pepper
- 6 cups French bread
- 1 ½ teaspoon smoked paprika
- 6 cups chicken broth
- 1 tablespoon olive oil
- 6 cloves garlic
- 2 ounces ham
- ¼ cup extra virgin olive oil

Method:
1. Preheat the oven to 350 degrees Fahrenheit.
2. Place the Sourdough bread on the baking tray that has been prepared.
3. Cook until crispy in a preheated oven.
4. In a large saucepan over medium heat, warm ¼ cup canola oil.
5. Cover and stir for 1 minute, or until ham is cooked through.
6. Cook for another minute after adding 1 to 2 teaspoons of parmesan.
7. Pour the chicken broth into the bread combination and whisk in the cayenne pepper, pepper, and garlic powder.
8. Bring to the boil, then decrease to low heat and whisk in the parsley.
9. Crack each egg into a shallow saucepan or cup.
10. With a spoon, make four downturns in the bread on the edge of the stew.
11. Pour the soup into bowls and finish with an egg.

6.10 Rustic Spanish Chicken Casserole

Cooking Time: 1 hour 20 minutes
Serving Size: 6

Ingredients:

- ½ teaspoon cayenne pepper
- 1 cup basil leaves
- 1 teaspoon dried oregano
- ½ teaspoon smoked paprika
- 1 cup stuffed pimento olives
- 1 carrot, diced
- 1 red bell pepper
- 2 tablespoon tomato paste
- 1 can cannellini beans
- ½ cup chicken stock
- 1 tablespoon olive oil
- 8 chicken thigh cutlets
- 2 cans tomatoes
- 3 garlic cloves
- 1 white onion

Method:

1. Preheat the oven to 180 degrees Celsius.
2. In a huge slow cooker, heat the oil over moderate flame.
3. For a few minutes, sauté the cloves and vegetables until they are translucent.

4. Cook for a few minutes after adding the chicken thighs.
5. With the exception of the basil leaves, combine all of the remaining ingredients in a mixing bowl.
6. 5 minutes on top of the burner, heat until softly bubbling.
7. Preheat the oven to 350°F and bake for 45 minutes on average.
8. Serve with carrots or cabbage rice.

6.11 Summer Spanish Salad

Cooking Time: 10 minutes

Serving Size: 2

Ingredients:

- 3 tablespoons olive oil
- 2 tablespoon red wine vinegar
- A pinch of cumin
- ½ teaspoon salt
- 2 large tomatoes
- 1 large green pepper
- 2 cloves garlic minced
- 1 medium onion
- 1 large cucumber

Method:

1. Dip the onions in water after cutting them into small cubes.

2. Position the tomatoes, celery, and peppers in a cup and chop them up.
3. Drain the vegetables and combine them with the remaining ingredients.
4. In a separate small cup, combine the remaining olive oil, vinegar, and salt, then stir in the garlic paste.
5. Toss the salad with the dressing and toss well.
6. Cover and store in the refrigerator.

6.12 Spanish Tuna and Potato Salad Recipe

Cooking Time: 24 minutes

Serving Size: 8

Ingredients:

- 3 tablespoon white wine vinegar
- 6 oz. spring greens
- ½ teaspoon red pepper flakes
- ⅓ cup Greek olive oil
- 1 teaspoon smoked paprika
- ¾ teaspoon cumin
- 3 large garlic cloves
- Salt and pepper
- 12 oz. fingerling potatoes
- ⅓ cup pearl red onions
- 15 oz. can quality tuna
- 6 oz. small tomatoes
- 10 oz. French green beans

Method:

1. Fill a big pot halfway with water and add the fingerling vegetables.
2. Cook for ten minutes at a low temperature.
3. Fill a wide bowl halfway with ice water and place it next to the pot.
4. Add green beans to the hot water in the same frying pan.
5. Cook for about four minutes.
6. Wash the green beans and instantly placed them in the ice water bowl.
7. Green beans, peppers, tomatoes, fish, and garlic are added to the pot.
8. Add Salt, powder, parmesan, cumin, and ground red pepper to taste.
9. Toss all together gently to ensure that all of the components are properly coated.
10. Taste and change seasoning, if necessary, by adding more smoked paprika, cilantro, or smashed red pepper.

6.13 Spanish Style Albondigas

Cooking Time: 2 hours 20 minutes

Serving Size: 4

Ingredients:
- 1 can plum tomatoes
- 2 tablespoons olive oil
- 1 cup white wine
- 2 tablespoons tomato puree
- ¼ teaspoon coriander

- 2 grinds black pepper
- ⅔ pound beef
- 1 ½ teaspoons basil
- 1 ½ teaspoons oregano
- ⅓ pound pork
- 2 tablespoons celery
- 1 clove garlic
- 2 tablespoons carrot
- 3 ½ ounces pancetta
- 3 tablespoons onion
- 3 ½ ounces white bread crumbs
- 2 tablespoons olive oil
- 2 tablespoons red bell pepper
- 2 dashes Worcestershire sauce
- Salt and pepper
- 2 tablespoons green onion
- 1 tablespoon fresh parsley
- 1 clove garlic
- 2 tablespoons fresh oregano

Method:

1. In a mixing bowl, combine ground beef, pork belly, spring onions, oregano, tarragon, garlic, Balsamic vinegar, salt, and black pepper.
2. Slowly stir in the breadcrumbs until the meat mixture reaches the perfect consistency.
3. Freezer meatballs for at least 30 minutes after wrapping them in cling film.

4. In a big saucepan, steam 2 tablespoons olive oil on medium-high heat.
5. In a hot skillet, continue cooking pancetta until it is golden brown, about four minutes. Toss in the vegetables and seasoning.
6. In a wide skillet, steam two tablespoons of oil over medium heat.
7. 6 to 10 minutes, continue cooking meatballs in hot oil quantities until uniformly browned and heated through.
8. Transfer the meatballs softly into the boiling sauce and cook together until the meatballs are thoroughly cooked.

6.14 Pontevedra-Style Spanish Chicken

Cooking Time: 1 hour 25 minutes
Serving Size: 6

Ingredients:

- ¼ cup Spanish smoked paprika
- Salt and black pepper
- ½ cup butter
- 1 head roasted garlic
- 2 cups olive oil
- 1 whole chicken

Method:

1. Preheat the oven to 350 degrees Fahrenheit.
2. Position the meat pieces skin-side up in a casserole dish.
3. Over the chicken, drizzle the sour cream and icing sugar.

4. Season the bits with salt and black pepper and chopped roasted garlic, parmesan, and tarragon.
5. Roast for thirty minutes in a dry pan.
6. Fry the chicken parts skin-side up until the chicken is cooked through and the meat is crisp.
7. Offer the chicken parts with a serving sauce on the side.

6.15 Spanish Cold Tomato Soup

Cooking Time: 25 minutes
Serving Size: 4
Ingredients:
- 2 hardboiled eggs
- Diced serrano ham
- A splash of sherry vinegar
- A pinch of salt
- 8 medium tomatoes
- 1 cup olive oil again
- 1 clove of garlic
- 1 medium baguette

Method:
1. Carry a big pot of salted water to a boil on the burner.
2. In the base of each tomato, make a small symbol.
3. Remove the cores from the tomatoes and mix everything else.
4. Use a high-powered blender, combine all ingredients.

5. Remove the "guts" from your baguette and toss them in with the blended vegetables.
6. Mix in the drop of vinegar, pepper, and garlic until the soup has even consistency.
7. Mix in 1 hardboiled egg until completely combined.
8. Offer in big containers with toppings of diced poblano pepper and diced ham. Serve chilled.

6.16 Spicy Spanish Meatballs

Cooking Time: 35 minutes

Serving Size: 4

Ingredients:

Spanish Meatballs

- 2 ½ teaspoon smoked paprika
- ¼ cup olive oil
- 2 clove garlic
- 1 egg yolk
- 2 tablespoon milk
- 500 grams beef
- ½ cup breadcrumbs

Smoked Paprika Tomato Sauce

- ½ teaspoon smoked paprika
- 500 grams tomatoes
- 3 cloves garlic
- 1 bay leaf
- 1 onion

- 1 tablespoon olive oil

Method:

1. Soak the breadcrumbs in dairy for five minutes before pressing out any remaining water.
2. Add salt and pepper to taste.
3. Make 12 balls out of the flour mix and place them on a table to work with.
4. In a large skillet, heat the oil over medium heat.
5. Heat the meatballs for four minutes, rotating once or until golden brown.
6. Heat for about four minutes with the spray of excess oil, onions, ginger, and bay leaf.
7. Wait for another minute till the paprika is aromatic.
8. Transfer the meatballs to the bowl after stirring in the tomatoes.
9. Transfer to a serving bowl and serve right away.

6.17 Sizzling Spanish Garlic Prawns

Cooking Time: 13 minutes

Serving Size: 6

Ingredients:

- 6 garlic cloves
- 6 tablespoons dry sherry
- 1 teaspoon chili flakes
- 4 tablespoons olive oil
- 3 tablespoons parsley
- 900g raw king prawns

Method:

1. Preheat the oven to 220 degrees Celsius.
2. Cut the prawns lengthwise but not through it and cut the vein to flap the shrimp.
3. Use six small oven tray dishes or one big one to separate the shrimp, garlic, chili or pimento, brandy, and balsamic vinegar.
4. Cook for 12 to 15 minutes until it is red and piping hot, based on the pan or pots' size.
5. Serve with toasted bread and citrus wedges, garnished with parsley.

6.18 Super Tasty Spanish Roast Chicken

Cooking Time: 1 hour 40 minutes

Serving Size: 8

Ingredients:

- Olive oil
- 2 cloves garlic
- Freshly ground black pepper
- 300g Iberico chorizo sausage
- 2kg chicken
- Sea salt
- 1.6kg potatoes
- 1 handful parsley
- 4 lemons

Method:

1. Heat your oven to 220°C, and put your vegetables in a large pan of boiling water containing two lemons and simmer for five minutes.

2. Take the leaves from the tarragon stalks and set them aside.
3. Fill the meat with the tarragon stalks and warm lemons.
4. Position the potato in the center of the baking parchment, then the poultry on top and the pancetta on top of that.
5. Whereas the chicken and vegetables are frying, make the gremolata, as the Italians name it.
6. Chop the poultry and serve with the potatoes on eight plates.

6.19 Spanish-Inspired Tomato Salad

Cooking Time: 40 minutes

Serving Size: 8

Ingredients:
- 16 caper berries
- 6 anchovy fillets
- 3 pounds tomatoes
- 1 cup parsley
- ½ teaspoon sugar
- ¼ teaspoon salt
- 1/3 cup olive oil
- 3 tablespoons sherry vinegar
- 1 teaspoon pepper
- 1 teaspoon paprika
- 1 cup fresh breadcrumbs
- 5 cloves garlic

Method:

1. In a large saucepan, warm 1/3 cup oil over moderate flame.
2. Cook, occasionally stirring, for about 20 seconds, just until the citrus is spicy and piping hot but not crispy.
3. In the same pan, heat and cook two tablespoons of oil over moderate flame.
4. Cook, constantly stirring, until the breadcrumbs are crisp and lightly browned, about five minutes.
5. In a mixing bowl, combine the garlic-paprika oil, mustard, spice, cinnamon, and salt.
6. Gently whisk in the onions, tarragon, caper fruit, and minced anchovies.
7. Serve the tomato salad on a large plate with the fried cornmeal on top.

6.20 Fruity Spanish Tapas

Cooking Time: 30 minutes

Serving Size: 4

Ingredients:

- 50g vegetarian manchego
- 1 tablespoon chives
- 1 tablespoon garlic oil
- 1 Pink Lady apple
- ¼ ciabatta

Method:

1. Trim the edges of the ciabatta blocks so they sit flat on a surface.
2. Heat a baking tray to a high temperature.

3. Grill the ciabatta pieces for 2-3 minutes, rotating once, until finely charred all over.
4. Remove the board from the oven and place it on top of it.
5. Heat for 2-3 minutes, rotating halfway, till the apple slices are slightly charred.
6. To combine, place two slices of fruit, a cheese slice, and a sprinkling of chives on each cube of bread.
7. Serve after securing with a toothpick.

Conclusion

Tapas can be eaten in a variety of ways. You'll probably wind up buying a lot of small dishes and exchanging them when you go out for tapas. This route, you can sample a variety of dishes at once. Tapas are small plates of meals available with small pieces of bread, and they reflect the best fresh foods from different parts of Spain in Madrid. Poblano Jamón Tapas are distinctive to each country. Queso manchego (a spreadable cheese in Spain's La Mancha area) is common in the southern coast center, while tapas with la morcilla (sausage) is popular in the north. Tapas can typically cost from 50 cents to four euros, based on the tapa. Even with the same tapa, prices vary based on the jamón (ham) location you request. Tapas are the nutrition purgatory; they are there to fill in the holes in your day. It does not complement or substitute for a meal, apart from an appetizer. They are sold at Tasca bars, where people indulge in these delicacies before lunch or dinner. Tapas would most probably be served in the evenings before dinners when you visit Spain. The excitement and the delicious food and drinks will hold you for more. So give these tapas ideas a try, and you'll fall in love with the flavor of these delectable tapas.

Pescatarian
COOKBOOK

70 Easy Recipes For Mediterranean Dishes With Fish And Seafood

---

Emma Yang

© Copyright 2021 by Emma Yang - All rights reserved.

This document is geared towards providing exact and reliable information in regard to the topic and issue covered. The publication is sold with the idea that the publisher is not required to render accounting, officially permitted, or otherwise, qualified services. If advice is necessary, legal or professional, a practiced individual in the profession should be ordered.

From a Declaration of Principles which was accepted and approved equally by a Committee of the American Bar Association and a Committee of Publishers and Associations.

In no way is it legal to reproduce, duplicate, or transmit any part of this document in either electronic means or in printed format. Recording of this publication is strictly prohibited and any storage of this document is not allowed unless with written permission from the publisher. All rights reserved.

The information provided herein is stated to be truthful and consistent, in that any liability, in terms of inattention or otherwise, by any usage or abuse of any policies, processes, or directions contained within is the solitary and utter responsibility of the recipient reader. Under no circumstances will any legal responsibility or blame be held against the publisher for any reparation, damages, or monetary loss due to the information herein, either directly or indirectly.

Respective authors own all copyrights not held by the publisher.

The information herein is offered for informational purposes solely and is universal as so. The presentation of the information is without contract or any type of guarantee assurance.

The trademarks that are used are without any consent, and the publication of the trademark is without permission or backing by the trademark owner. All trademarks and brands within this book are for clarifying purposes only and are owned by the owners themselves, not affiliated with this document.

Contents

INTRODUCTION 110

CHAPTER 1: HEALTHY FISH AND SEAFOOD BREAKFAST RECIPES 112

1.1 Smoked Salmon Baked Eggs in Avocado 112

1.2 Smoked Salmon and Dill Waffles 113

1.3 Simple Shrimp Scramble 115

1.4 Bacon Lobster Omelet 116

1.5 Seafood Bake with Crispy Hash Brown Topping 117

1.6 Lobster Breakfast Sandwich 118

1.7 Shrimp and Spinach Omelette 119

1.8 Brunchy Fish and Waffles 120

1.9 Smoked Salmon Hash 123

1.10 Alaska Salmon Frittata 125

CHAPTER 2: HEALTHY FISH AND SEAFOOD LUNCH AND DINNER 127

2.1 Furikake Salmon Bowls 128

2.2 Pan-Seared Halibut over Lemony Zucchini Noodles 131

2.3 Rum-Glazed Shrimp 133

2.4 Air Fryer Salmon 134

2.5 Garlicky Shrimp Alfredo Bake 135

2.6 Oysters Rockefeller 136

2.7 Bruschetta Salmon 138

2.8 Creamed Spinach Stuffed Salmon 140

2.9 Shrimp Alfredo 142

2.10 Baked Swordfish...143

2.11 Mussels with Tomatoes and Garlic 145

2.12 Easy Shrimp Fajitas 146

2.13 BBQ Salmon and Brussels Bake 147

2.14 Shrimp Fried Rice 149

2.15 Fish Stick Tacos...151

2.16 Coconut Shrimp Curry..154

2.17 Fish Packets with Caper Butter and Snap Peas.................................156

2.18 Red Curry Shrimp and Noodles 157

2.19 Salmon and Ginger Rice Bowl 159

2.20 Shrimp and Zucchini Scampi 160

2.21 French-Inspired Tuna Nicoise...162

2.22 One Pan Mustard Glazed Salmon 163

2.23 Grilled Stuffed Rainbow Trout 165

2.24 Salmon and Beets with Yogurt Sauce over Watercress 167

2.25 Lobster-Noodle Casserole 168

2.26 Lobster Mac and Cheese Recipe 170

2.27 Lemon-Parmesan Angel Hair Pasta with Shrimp 173

2.28 Sheet Pan Shrimp with Broccoli and Tomatoes 174

2.29 Garlic Butter Shrimp 176

2.30 Grilled Lobster Tails with Herb Garlic Butter 178

2.31 Salmon with Chickpeas and Spinach 179

CHAPTER 3: HEALTHY FISH AND SEAFOOD SNACKS AND SALADS RECIPES 181

3.1 Crab Cakes 181

3.2 Shrimp Ceviche 183

3.3 Salmon Patties 184

3.4: Crab Hush Puppies 186

3.5 Baked Clams 188

3.6 General Tso's Shrimp 'n Broccoli 190

3.7 Bang Bang Shrimp 191

3.8 Simple Ceviche Recipe 193

3.9 Smoked Salmon, Avocado, and Fennel Salad 195

3.10 Cilantro-Lime Shrimp Salad 196

3.11 Shrimp Salad 198

3.12 Smoked Salmon and Oatmeal Salad 199

3.13 Pan Seared Scallops and Quinoa Salad 201

3.14 Shrimp and Avocado Taco Salad 203

3.15 Crab and Shrimp Salad with Mango 205

3.16 Shoyu Ahi Poke Recipe 207

CHAPTER 4: HEALTHY FISH AND SEAFOOD SOUP RECIPES 208

4.1 Lobster Bisque 208

4.2 Italian Fish Stew 211

4.3 Asian Shrimp and Vegetable Soup 213

4.4 Salmon Chowder 215

4.5 Seafood Cioppino 217

4.6 Wild Rice, Shrimp & Fennel Soup 219

4.7 Seafood Stew 221

4.8 Brazilian Fish Stew 224

4.9 Clam Chowder 226

4.10 Crab-Okra Gumbo 228

4.11 Crab Bisque 230

4.12 Slow-Cooked Shrimp and Scallop Soup 232

4.13 Lemon Salmon Soup 233

CONCLUSION 235

Introduction

Cutting meat from your eating regimen may appear to be an immense change. Adopting a Pescatarian diet is quite easy. The key is to never cause yourself to feel like you are forfeiting something or limiting yourself. A Pescatarian diet avoids red meat, poultry, sheep, and pork. You will find vegetables, grains, natural products, beans, cheddar, eggs, and yogurt in a Pescatarian diet. It puts an accentuation on fish and shellfish as a rich source of protein.

Pescatarian diet leads to healthy eating habits and a lifestyle. How we feed our bodies affects our general prosperity. A plant-based eating regimen based on healthy food sources and a fish-driven eating routine loaded with protein has many advantages because of the collaboration of plants and fish.

A Pescatarian diet is protein-stuffed and rich in omega-3s. It decreases congestive cardiovascular breakdown and coronary illness. Sleek fish, specifically (think sardines, mackerel, or salmon), are stacked in unsaturated fats. It advances sufficient omega-3s. Eating fish and seafood expands your admission of omega-3s, which may offer various advantages—from lessening aggravation in the body to advancing cerebrum wellbeing. Notwithstanding greasy fish, chia seeds, flaxseeds, or pecans are incredible plant-based wellsprings of omega-3s.

An eating regimen wealthy in fish and seafood would help supply this imperative supplement. Fish offers a wellspring of complete protein. The intake of Pescatarian food sources can guarantee ideal protein consumption.

Likewise, in contrast to red meat, it is low in soaked fat and better for your heart and pulse hazard. If you are worried about heart wellbeing or have a background marked by coronary illness in your family, you may profit by going Pescatarian.

People choose a Pescatarian diet to lessen their ecological effects by eating fish and plant-based food varieties. It can diminish effects on water biological systems, territory obliteration, undermined species, and overfishing.

The 'Pescatarian Cookbook' offers you 70 healthy recipes that you can have for your Pescatarian diet. The Pescatarian Cookbook is your go-to reference to make the Pescatarian diet a supportable and fulfilling way of life.

Chapter 1: Healthy Fish and Seafood Breakfast Recipes

In a Pescatarian diet, breakfast foods easily fit in the meal plan. Here are some of the healthy and tasty fish and seafood breakfast recipes that you can easily make at home with any difficulty:

1.1 Smoked Salmon Baked Eggs in Avocado

Preparation Time: 10 minutes
Cooking Time: 15 minutes
Serving: 6

Ingredients:

- 3 avocado
- 6 eggs
- 3 slices smoked salmon
- 1 tbsp. of finely chopped Chives
- 1 pinch cayenne pepper
- Toasted bread, for serving

Instructions:
1. Heat oven to 180°C.
2. Cut avocados. Put them onto a baking plate.
3. Add salmon to each, and afterward add the egg yolks. Beat the egg whites.

4. Add cayenne pepper and heat for ten minutes, or until the whites have set. Disperse over the chives and a touch of cayenne. Present with toasted bread.

1.2 Smoked Salmon and Dill Waffles

Preparation Time: 40 minutes

Cooking Time: 40 minutes

Serving: 4

Ingredients:

- For Dill Waffles:
- 1 tbsp. granulated sugar
- 1/2 tbsp. baking powder
- 1/2 tsp. table salt
- 3/4 tsp. black pepper
- 1 egg
- 1/4 cup of melted unsalted butter
- 2 tbsp. milk
- 3/4 cup of seltzer
- 2 tbsp. of fresh dill
- For Poached Eggs:
- 4 large eggs
- 2 tsp. white vinegar
- For Serving:

- 8 slices of smoked salmon
- 1/2 cup of Hollandaise Sauce
- Fresh dill, for garnishing

Instructions:

1. In a bowl, whisk together flour, baking powder, sugar, pepper, and salt.
2. Mix egg yolk, dill, milk, seltzer, and butter.
3. In a bowl, beat the egg.
4. Crease egg whites into the waffle maker just until streaks vanish.
5. Preheat the stove to 200°F.
6. Preheat and add a few drops of oil to your waffle iron.
7. Cook waffles until colored and fresh.
8. Transfer waffles in a layer to a wire rack-lined preparing sheet and spot in the oven to keep warm.
9. Fill a bowl with hot water and cover to keep warm.
10. Fill a ten to twelve-inch width, a straight-sided dish with around two cups of water.
11. Mix in vinegar.
12. Cook the eggs for three to four minutes.
13. Move eggs to the bowl of heated water while you make the hollandaise.
14. Spot two cuts of smoked salmon on top of a warm waffle. Eliminate eggs from the warm water with a spoon.

15. Add the eggs to salmon.
16. Add hollandaise sauce.
17. Add dill, and serve.

1.3 Simple Shrimp Scramble

Preparation Time: 15 minutes
Cooking Time: 10 minutes
Serving: 4

Ingredients:

- 1 onion
- 1/4 cup of green pepper
- 1 minced garlic clove
- 3 tbsp. butter, divided
- 1 package of frozen salad shrimp, cooked
- 8 eggs
- 1/2 tsp. salt
- 1/4 tsp. pepper
- 1 cup of cheddar cheese

Instructions:

1. In a huge skillet, sauté the green pepper, onion, and garlic in one tbsp. of butter. Mix in shrimp. Take out in a bowl and keep warm.

2. In a similar skillet, dissolve the remaining butter over medium heat. Add eggs; cook, and mix until totally set. Mix in the shrimp blend, pepper and salt.
3. Sprinkle with cheddar.
4. Cover and let it set for three to five minutes.

1.4 Bacon Lobster Omelet

Preparation Time: 10 minutes
Cooking Time: 10 minutes
Serving: 1

Ingredients:

- 1/4 cup lobster meat
- 1 1/2 cup sour cream
- 1 tsp. of dijon mustard
- 2 eggs
- 1 tbsp. Of water
- 1 tbsp. green onions
- 1/2 tsp. Of dried tarragon
- 1 tsp. of butter
- Salt and pepper, to taste

Instructions:

1. In a small bowl, add sour cream and mustard.

2. In a medium bowl, combine green onions, one egg, tarragon and pepper and salt.
3. Add butter in a skillet, add egg, and then blend and cook till set.
4. Heat butter in a skillet, add the mixture of egg and cook till set.
5. Add sour cream in egg mixture. Blend it and add the lobster meat.
6. Crease another portion of eggs over the lobster side.
7. Serve while warm.

1.5 Seafood Bake with Crispy Hash Brown Topping

Preparation Time: 20 minutes

Cooking Time: 20 minutes

Serving: 4

Ingredients:

- 1 cup of sour cream
- 1 tbsp. Of cornstarch
- 2 tsp. Of lemon zest
- 1 tbsp. Of Dijon mustard
- Pepper, to taste
- Kosher salt, to taste
- 1 1/2 lb. Of mixed seafood
- 1 package of leaf spinach

- 2 cup of frozen hash browns

Instructions:

1. Heat stove to 425⁰ F. In a huge bowl, whisk together the sour cream, mustard, cornstarch, lemon zing, and half tsp. each pepper and salt.
2. Add the fish to the cream blend.
3. Add spinach into the mixture of fish.
4. Split between four shallow, one-cup preparing dishes.
5. Add hash browns and brush with olive oil. Cook for twenty to twenty-five minutes.
6. Serve and enjoy.

1.6 Lobster Breakfast Sandwich

Preparation Time: 5 minutes
Cooking Time: 10 minutes
Serving: 4

Ingredients:

- 4 brioche of sandwich buns
- 1 creamy egg
- 1 tsp. of olive oil
- 18 asparagus spears
- 4 lobster tails
- 1 tsp. of chopped fresh chives

Instructions:

1. Part out arranged velvety fried eggs on brioche sandwich buns.
2. Put asparagus sticks softly in olive oil.
3. Put it on the fried eggs, then top with chilled split lobster tail. Sprinkle chives to taste and serve.

1.7 Shrimp and Spinach Omelette

Preparation Time: 5 minutes

Cooking Time: 5 minutes

Serving: 2

Ingredients:

- 10 shrimp
- 6 large eggs
- 1 sprig parsley
- 4 tomatoes
- 1/4 onion
- 1 handful of spinach
- 1 tbsp. of sriracha salt
- 1/4 tsp. of cayenne

Instructions:
1. Cut onion and grape tomatoes.
2. Add onion and salt in a pan.
3. Simultaneously, place the grape tomatoes to broil a bit.
4. When the onions are cooked, toss in spinach, let it wither.
5. Add shrimp.
6. Cook eggs and cover the dish, so the omelet cooks well.
7. Cook for around six to eight minutes.
8. When a slim film of white is covering the yolks, eggs are prepared.
9. Add parsley over it.
10. Serve and enjoy.

1.8 Brunchy Fish and Waffles

Preparation Time: 10 minutes

Cooking Time: 20 minutes

Serving: 4

Ingredients:

- 1 package of Fish Fillets
- 4 Belgian Waffles
- 4 eggs
- 2 tbsp. Of unsalted butter
- One pinch of pepper and pinch of salt
- 1 cup maple syrup
- 1 tbsp. Of fish sauce
- 1/2 cup of honey
- 1 thinly sliced jalapeño
- 1 inch slice fresh ginger
- 2 tsp. Of orange zest
- 1/4 tsp. Of white pepper

Instructions:

1. In a pan over medium-low heat, add butter, maple syrup, fish sauce, honey, ginger, and orange zest, and cook for ten minutes.

2. Let it cool while preparing both fish and waffles as per instructions on the package.

3. Heat butter in a pan.

4. Add eggs and cook until whites have completely set—season with pepper and salt.

5. For serving, place one toasted waffle on a plate. Top with one egg. Stack two fish filets on top of the egg, inclining toward each other to try not to break the yolk.

6. Sprinkle some Jalapeño Maple syrup, and serve.

1.9 Smoked Salmon Hash

Preparation Time: 10 minutes
Cooking Time: 10 minutes
Serving: 2

Ingredients:

- 2 tbsp. olive oil
- 3 red potatoes
- 1 chopped yellow onion
- 1 bell pepper, green
- Kosher salt and black pepper
- 2 tsp. fresh chives, thinly sliced
- 1 1/2 tsp. Of lemon juice
- 2/3 cup sour cream
- 1/2 tsp. Of Dijon mustard
- One salmon fillet

Instructions:

1. Heat the oil in a nonstick skillet over a medium-high flame. Add the onions, potatoes, chime pepper, pepper, and salt, and cook while regularly mixing, until earthy colored, around ten minutes.
2. Cook until the potatoes are delicate, around fifteen minutes more; season to taste with pepper and salt.

3. In the meantime, put sour cream, one tbsp. chives, half tbsp. lemon juice, mustard, half tsp. of salt, and one-eighth tsp. of pepper.
4. Add salmon and one tbsp. lemon juice and keep cooking until warmed through, around two minutes more.
5. Move the hash to plates. Add the one tbsp. of chives and serve with sour cream.
6. Present it with a poached egg on top.

1.10 Alaska Salmon Frittata

Preparation Time: 20 minutes
Cooking Time: 14
Serving: 8

Ingredients:

- 12 beaten eggs
- 1 tbsp. olive oil
- 1 cup of sliced sweet peppers
- 2 1/2 cups broccoli florets
- 1/2 cup of diced onion
- 1 cup salmon
- 1/2 cup frozen peas
- Ground pepper, to taste
- Salt, to taste

Instructions:
1. Preheat broiler to 375°F
2. Add the broccoli florets, diced onion, cut small-scale sweet peppers in oil.
3. Season with ocean salt and ground dark pepper.
4. Mix in the frozen peas and smoked salmon.
5. Pour in the beaten eggs. Mix well.

6. Keep cooking the frittata, without blending, over the burner for an extra sixty seconds just until the external edge of the frittata starts to set.

7. Place the hot skillet on the stove; cook for ten to fourteen minutes, just until the eggs are set.

8. Allow the frittata to set for five minutes before cutting. Serve hot or cold.

Chapter 2: Healthy Fish and Seafood Lunch and Dinner

Pescatarian lunch and dinner recipes are full of healthy proteins and flavors. There are many varieties of fish and seafood recipes that can be eaten during lunch and dinner time. Following are given some of these recipes that you can try at home:

2.1 Furikake Salmon Bowls

Preparation Time: 10 minutes
Cooking Time: 20 minutes
Serving: 2

Ingredients:

- For Salmon:
- 1 to 2 tbsp. sesame oil
- 1 Pinch pepper, salt and chili flakes
- 8 to 10 ounces of salmon
- 4 ounces of shiitake mushrooms
- For Sauce:
- 3 tbsp. Of soy sauce
- 3 tbsp. Mirin
- 1 tbsp. Furikake
- 1/2 to 2 cups of cooked rice
- 2 bunches of cabbage
- 1 large avocado
- For toppings:
- Scallions
- Cucumber
- Furikake
- Stew pieces

Instructions:

1. Mix mirin and soy sauce in a small bowl.
2. Heat sesame oil in a huge skillet over medium-high heat. Season with pepper and salt.
3. Add the mushrooms and salmon and cook. Turn the heat off, allowing the skillet to cool somewhat.
4. Add sauce over the salmon and mushrooms.
5. Divide rice between two dishes. Sprinkle it with furikake.
6. Put cabbage, avocado wedges, and some other veggies in the bowl.
7. Top with burned salmon and mushrooms, and sprinkle it with Furikake, spooning the excess sauce over the avocado and cabbage.
8. Serve immediately.

2.2 Pan-Seared Halibut over Lemony Zucchini Noodles

Preparation Time: 30 minutes
Cooking Time: 30 minutes
Serving: 2

Ingredients:

- 8 to 10 ounces halibut
- 1 smashed garlic clove
- 1 to 2 tbsp. olive oil
- Pepper, to taste
- Salt, to taste
- For Noodles:
- 1 tbsp. olive oil
- 1 thinly sliced fat shallot
- 3 chopped garlic cloves
- 12 to 16 ounces of zucchini noodles
- pepper, to taste
- Salt, to taste
- 2 tsp. lemon zest
- ½ cup of chopped Italian parsley
- 1 tbsp. Of lemon juice

Instructions:

1. Preheat oven to 375 F. Add garlic cloves in the tray.
2. Season fish with salt and pepper.
3. Place in the oven for about three to six minutes.
4. In a skillet, heat more oil over medium heat and add shallots and garlic, blending until mellowed and fragrant, around three minutes.
5. Add zucchini noodles and season with pepper and salt. Sauté until noodles mellow, around four minutes.
6. Add lemon zing, new parsley, and a crush of lemon. Add salt and lemon. Split between two dishes and top with the halibut.
7. Top with cherry tomatoes, bean stew chips, and pecorino cheddar.

2.3 Rum-Glazed Shrimp

Preparation Time: 10 minutes
Cooking Time: 35 minutes
Serving: 4

Ingredients:

- 1 1/2 lb. Of peeled shrimp
- 3 tbsp. Of olive oil
- 1/3 cup of chili sauce
- 1/4 cup of soy sauce
- 1/4 cup of Rum
- 2 minced cloves garlic
- 1 lime
- 1/2 tsp. Of red pepper flakes
- 1 thinly sliced green onion, to garnish

Instructions:

1. Add shrimp in a bowl.
2. In a bowl, add olive oil, sweet bean stew sauce, soy sauce, rum, garlic, lime juice, and red pepper drops.
3. Let marinate in the cooler for fifteen to thirty minutes.
4. Add shrimp in the oil and cook on one side for around two minutes.

5. Add green onions and serve.

2.4 Air Fryer Salmon

Preparation Time: 7 minutes
Cooking Time: 12 minutes
Serving: 5

Ingredients:

- 2 wild salmon fillets
- 2 tsps. of tsp. avocado oil
- 2 tsps. of paprika
- Black pepper, to taste
- Salt, to taste
- Lemon wedges

Instructions:
1. Eliminate any bones from salmon and set aside for one hour.
2. Rub each fillet with olive oil and season with paprika, salt and pepper.
3. Put fillets in the air fryer at 390 degrees for seven minutes.
4. When the time is over, check fillets with a fork to ensure they are done.

2.5 Garlicky Shrimp Alfredo Bake

Preparation Time: 20 minutes
Cooking Time: 20 minutes
Serving: 4

Ingredients:

- 12 ounces of penne
- 3 minced cloves garlic
- 1 lb. Of raw shrimp
- 3 tbsp. Of divided butter
- 2 tbsp. Of chopped parsley
- Kosher salt, to taste
- 2 tbsp. of flour
- 1/4 cup of chicken broth
- 3/4 cup of milk
- 1cup of shredded mozzarella
- 1/4 cup of grated Parmesan
- Black pepper, to taste
- 1 cup of chopped tomatoes

Instructions:
1. Preheat the stove to 350°F.
2. In a huge pot of water, prepare penne as per instructions on the package.

3. Add shrimp, garlic, and parsley in the oil and season with salt. Cook until the shrimp is pink.
4. Add two tablespoon butter and flour and cook for about one minute.
5. Put milk and stock in it. Mix in mozzarella and Parmesan, pepper, and with salt.
6. Add tomatoes, cooked penne, and shrimp, and throw until consolidated.
7. Sprinkle with mozzarella and two tbsp. parmesan and heat until melted, five to seven minutes.
8. Sprinkle parsley before serving.

2.6 Oysters Rockefeller

Preparation Time: 15 minutes
Cooking Time: 1 hour
Serving: 2 dozen

Ingredients:

- 1 finely chopped medium onion
- 1/2 cup of cubed butter
- 1 package of fresh spinach
- 1 cup of Romano cheese
- 1 tbsp. lemon juice
- 1/8 tsp. pepper
- 2 pounds of kosher salt
- 3 dozen of fresh oysters

Instructions:

1. In a skillet, sauté onion. Add spinach; cook and mix until withered. Eliminate from the heat; mix in cheddar, lemon juice and pepper.
2. Spread salt into two ungreased heating dishes. Add oysters in the base shell.
3. Add salt in the clamshells.
4. Top each with two teaspoons of spinach.
5. Prepare, uncovered, at 450° F until oysters are fully cooked, six to eight minutes. Serve.

2.7 Bruschetta Salmon

Preparation Time: 10 minutes
Cooking Time: 15 minutes
Serving: 4

Ingredients:

- 4 salmon fillets
- 1 tsp. Of dried oregano
- Kosher salt, to taste
- Black pepper, to taste
- 2 tbsp. Of olive oil
- 3 minced cloves garlic
- 2 minced shallots
- 3 cup of cherry tomatoes
- 1/2 lemon
- 1/4 cup of basil
- Parmesan, to serve
- Balsamic glaze
- Toppings:
- Tomatoes, red onion, avocado, jalapeño peppers, and coriander sprigs

Instructions:

1. Season salmon with oregano, salt and pepper.

2. Add salmon in the heated oil and cook for around six minutes.
3. Flip and cook for six minutes until the salmon is misty. Move to a plate.
4. Add remaining tablespoon olive oil to skillet, mix in garlic and shallots. Cook until garlic is fragrant.
5. Add tomatoes and season with salt and pepper.
6. Add lemon juice.
7. Serve salmon with tomato blend spooned on top. Top with basil and Parmesan, sprinkle with balsamic coating.

2.8 Creamed Spinach Stuffed Salmon

Preparation Time: 10 minutes
Cooking Time: 20 minutes
Serving: 2

Ingredients:

- For Salmon:
- 4 salmon fillets
- Pepper and salt, to season
- 2 tbsp. lemon juice
- 2 tbsp. olive oil
- 1 tbsp. unsalted butter
- For Filling:
- 4 ounces cream cheese
- 4 ounces frozen spinach
- 1/4 cup of parmesan cheese
- 2 tsp. minced garlic
- Pepper and salt, to taste
- For Garlic Butter:
- 1 tbsp. unsalted butter
- 1 tbsp. minced garlic
- 1 tbsp. lemon juice

Instructions:

1. Season the two sides with salt, pepper, one tablespoon olive oil, and lemon juice.
2. In a medium-sized bowl, add the spinach, cream cheddar, parmesan cheddar and garlic.
3. Add pepper and salt.
4. Heat butter and oil in a skillet over medium heat.
5. Add the salmon and fry for around six to seven minutes.
6. Cook the other side for around six to seven minutes.
7. Add the garlic and lemon juice; sauté until garlic is fragrant (around 30 seconds). Present with the salmon.

2.9 Shrimp Alfredo

Preparation Time: 30 minutes

Cooking Time: 10 minutes

Serving: 6

Ingredients:

- 10 ounces of fettuccine pasta
- 5 tbsp. butter
- 1 cup of heavy cream
- 3/4 cup of parmesan cheese
- Pepper, to taste
- Salt, to taste
- 1 pound of shrimp
- 1 tsp. minced garlic
- 2 tbsp. chopped parsley

Instructions:

1. Cook the pasta in salted water.
2. Add four tablespoons butter in a pot over medium-low heat.
3. Add the cream and stew for four to five minutes or until just thickened.
4. Add parmesan cheddar, blending consistently until cheddar has softened.
5. Add pepper and salt.
6. Heat one tablespoon butter in a huge skillet over medium-high heat.

7. Add the shrimp and season with salt and pepper.
8. Cook the shrimp for three to four minutes until shrimps are pink and obscure.
9. Add the garlic to the dish and cook for an extra thirty seconds.
10. Add pasta and alfredo sauce. Put the shrimp on top and sprinkle with parsley, and serve.

2.10 Baked Swordfish

Preparation Time: 5 minutes
Cooking Time: 22 minutes
Serving: 1

Ingredients:

- ½ pound of swordfish steak
- 2 tbsp. Of olive oil
- 1 tsp. Of garlic powder
- 2 lemons
- Sea salt, to taste
- 2-4 chopped green onions
- 2-4 tbsp. Of white wine
- Lemon slices, to garnish

Instructions:

1. Preheat stove at 375 degrees F (190.6 degrees C).

2. Utilize a profound, heating dish sufficiently huge to hold the swordfish steak.

First for the Marinade:

3. On the lower part of the heating dish, add a tablespoon of olive oil, and one entire lemon, sprinkle with half teaspoon of ground garlic powder.

4. Place swordfish steak on top of the main layer of marinade.

5. Sprinkle on top of the swordfish steak with some additional virgin olive oil, the leftover garlic powder and lemon.

6. Sprinkle some ocean salt on top of the steak. Add green onions. Put white wine on top, and let it sit for fifteen minutes to marinate.

7. Bake for eighteen to twenty two minutes, or until swordfish is white or completely cooked.

8. Add lemon sauce over the swordfish steak and serve.

2.11 Mussels with Tomatoes and Garlic

Preparation Time: 10 minutes
Cooking Time: 20 minutes
Serving: 4

Ingredients:

- 2 tbsp. of butter
- 1 chopped onion
- 3 minced cloves garlic
- 1 can of diced tomatoes
- 1/2 cup white wine
- 2 tbsp. Of chopped parsley
- Kosher salt, to taste
- Black pepper, to taste
- 2 lb. Of mussels
- Grilled bread, to serve
- 1 tsp. Kosher salt

Instructions:

1. In a pot over medium-low heat, warm the butter. Add onion and cook for five minutes. Add garlic and cook until fragrant.
2. Add diced tomatoes, wine, and parsley—season with salt and pepper.
3. Add mussels and stew until all shells are open.

4. Top with more parsley and present with barbecued bread.

2.12 Easy Shrimp Fajitas

Preparation Time: 5 minutes
Cooking Time: 12 minutes
Serving: 4

Ingredients:

- 1 tbsp. Of vegetable oil
- 2 cups of sliced red bell peppers yellow, orange, and red
- 1 thinly sliced onion
- 2 tsp. chili powder
- 1/2 tsp. ground cumin
- 1/4 tsp. garlic powder
- 1/4 tsp. onion powder
- 1/2 tsp. smoked paprika
- 2 tbsp. chopped cilantro
- 1 pound of large shrimp
- Lime wedges, to serve
- 4 tortillas
- Fajita toppings
- Pepper, to taste
- Salt, to taste

Instructions:
1. Heat the oil in a large pan over high heat.
2. Add the onion and peppers.
3. Season the vegetables with salt and pepper.
4. In a small bowl, mix stew powder, cumin, garlic powder, onion powder, smoked paprika, and salt and pepper to taste.
5. Add the shrimp and sprinkle the flavoring mix over the shrimp and vegetables.
6. Cook until shrimp are pink and misty.
7. Add cilantro and serve. Add lime wedges.
8. Serve the flour tortillas.

2.13 BBQ Salmon and Brussels Bake

Preparation Time: 10 minutes
Cooking Time: 20 minutes
Serving: 8

Ingredients:

- 2 tbsp. Of brown sugar
- 1 tsp. Of garlic powder
- 1 tsp. of onion powder
- 3 1/2 pounds of salmon
- 1 tsp. Of smoked paprika

- 1 1/4 lb. Of Brussels sprouts
- Chives

Instructions:

1. Preheat broiler to 450°F. Line two sheets with foil.
2. Mix sugar, one teaspoon garlic powder, one teaspoon onion powder, one teaspoon smoked paprika, and two tablespoons olive oil.
3. Divide one-fourth pound of Brussels sprouts.
4. Put sprouts on one sheet and add one tablespoon olive oil, one-fourth teaspoon salt, and one-fourth teaspoon pepper.
5. Cook sprouts for five minutes. While sprouts broil, prepare salmon.
6. Cut one side of salmon into ten filets. Brush the flavor, rub all over the salmon, and sprinkle salmon with one teaspoon of salt.
7. Mix Brussels.
8. Add salmon to the stove and cook for fifteen minutes.
9. Serve salmon with Brussels sprouts. Add chives on top.

2.14 Shrimp Fried Rice

Preparation Time: 30 minutes
Cooking Time: 10 minutes
Serving: 4

Ingredients:

- 3 tbsp. soy sauce
- 1 tbsp. sesame oil
- 1/2 tsp. ginger powder
- 1/2 tsp. white pepper
- 2 tbsp. olive oil
- 1 pound shrimp
- Kosher salt, to taste
- Black pepper, to taste
- 2 minced cloves garlic
- 1 diced onion
- 2 grated carrots
- 1/2 cup of frozen corn
- 1/2 cup of frozen peas
- 3 cups of cooked rice
- 2 diced green onions

Instructions:

1. In a small bowl, whisk together soy sauce, sesame oil, ginger powder, and white pepper.

2. Add shrimp in oil, and cook, until pink, around two to three minutes; add pepper and salt to taste.
3. Add garlic and onion to the skillet, and cook for around three to four minutes.
4. Mix carrots, corn, and peas, and cook, for three to four minutes.
5. Mix rice, green onions, and soy sauce combination. Cook for two minutes. Mix in shrimp.
6. Serve.

2.15 Fish Stick Tacos

Preparation Time: 10 minutes
Cooking Time: 30 minutes
Serving: 4

Ingredients:

- For Fish Stick Tacos:
- 16 Fish Sticks
- 8 corn tortillas
- 1/2 tsp. of garlic powder
- 1/2 tsp. Of smoked paprika
- 1/2 tsp. of onion powder
- 1/2 tsp. of cumin
- 1/2 tsp. of kosher salt
- 1/4 tsp. of cayenne pepper
- Cooking spray
- For Taco Slaw:
- 2 cups of purple cabbage
- 2 cups of shredded carrots
- 1/4 cup of cilantro chopped
- 3 chopped green onions
- 1/4 cup of pickled jalapeños
- 2 tbsp. of Greek yogurt
- 2 tsp. Of pickled jalapeño
- 1 lime

- Sea salt, to taste
- Pepper, to taste

Instructions:

1. Preheat the oven to 450 degrees F.
2. Add sliced cabbage, carrots, salted jalapeños, cilantro, and green onions to a medium bowl.
3. In a small bowl, add Greek yogurt, salted jalapeño juice, and the juice of one lime.
4. Add salt and pepper to taste.
5. Put aside.

For Fish Sticks Tacos:

6. Add garlic powder, onion powder, smoked paprika, cumin, salt, and cayenne pepper into a small bowl. Mix well.

7. Spray oil on the baking dish, and put sixteen fish sticks on it.

8. Place it in 450 degrees preheated stove for eighteen minutes. Flip it carefully.

9. While the fish sticks are preparing, heat eight corn tortillas.

10. When the fish sticks are done, form every taco by putting two fish sticks on top of every tortilla and taco slaw on top.

11. Serve and enjoy!

2.16 Coconut Shrimp Curry

Preparation Time: 15 minutes
Cooking Time: 20 minutes
Serving: 4

Ingredients:

For Shrimp Marinade:
- 1 lb. of shrimp
- 2 tbsp. of lemon juice
- ¼ tsp. of salt
- ¼ tsp. of black pepper
- ¼ tsp. of cayenne pepper

For the sauce:
- 1 tbsp. Of coconut oil
- 1 chopped onion
- 3 minced cloves garlic
- 1 tbsp. Of ginger minced
- ½ tsp. of black pepper
- ½ tsp. of salt, to taste
- ½ tsp. of turmeric
- 1 tsp. Of curry powder
- 2 tsp. of ground coriander
- 14 ounces diced tomatoes

- 13 ounce coconut milk
- 1 tbsp. of cilantro, to garnish
- Cooked rice to serve

Instructions:
1. In a small bowl, add shrimp with the ingredients of marinade. Cover with cling wrap, then refrigerate for almost ten minutes.
2. Add the onion in oil, cook for two to three minutes until the onion mollifies and gets clear.
3. Mix the ginger, garlic, salt, pepper, coriander, curry powder, and turmeric.
4. Add tomatoes, coconut milk, mix, and heat to the point of boiling. Cook for around five minutes.
5. Add the shrimp with the gathered juices from the marinade and cook for two minutes.
6. Serve with hot rice.

2.17 Fish Packets with Caper Butter and Snap Peas

Preparation Time: 10 minutes
Cooking Time: 25 minutes
Serving: 2

Ingredients:

- 3 tbsp. Of softened butter
- 3 tbsp. Chopped capers
- Kosher salt, to taste
- 1 lb. Of peas
- 1 thinly sliced lemon
- 3 fillets halibut
- Basil, to garnish

Instructions:

1. Mix capers, butter, and one-fourth teaspoon salt. Add lemon.
2. Top peas with fish filets. Sprinkle each filet with salt and speck with butter—overlap and crease foil edges to seal firmly.
3. Cook in a microwave while keeping it covered, on medium heat for twelve minutes. Serve with topping of basil.

2.18 Red Curry Shrimp and Noodles

Preparation Time: 20 minutes
Cooking Time: 16 minutes
Serving: 4

Ingredients:

- 3 tbsp. coconut oil
- 1/2 pound of raw shrimp
- ½ sliced sweet onion
- ½ sliced bell pepper, red
- 1/2 sliced bell pepper, orange
- 1/2 tsp. salt
- 1/2 tsp. pepper
- 2 minced garlic cloves
- 1/2 tsp. grated ginger
- 2 tbsp. red curry
- 1/3 cup of peas
- 1 can of coconut milk
- 1 can of coconut milk
- 6 ounces of rice noodles, cooked
- 3 tbsp. chopped cilantro
- 2 sliced green onions

Instructions:

1. Warm a huge skillet over medium heat and add two tablespoons of coconut oil. Include the shrimp and cook until hazy and pink on the two sides.
2. Sprinkle salt and pepper over it. Remove the shrimp and place it in a bowl.
3. Add the leftover coconut oil to the pot.
4. Add onion, pepper, and salt.
5. Cook for around five minutes.
6. Include the garlic, ginger, and curry glue. Cook for five minutes.
7. Put snap peas and coconut milk in it. Increase heat to the point of boiling, then lower it, cover and cook for five minutes.
8. Add shrimp and cilantro. Cook for five minutes.
9. To serve, place a small bunch of rice noodles in a bowl and cover with the shrimp curry.
10. Top with additional cilantro or green onions.

2.19 Salmon and Ginger Rice Bowl

Preparation Time: 10 minutes
Cooking Time: 30 minutes
Serving: 2

Ingredients:

- 1 cup of brown or white rice
- 2 tbsp. Of butter
- 3 salmon fillets
- 2 tsp. Of curry powder
- 1 tbsp. Of lemon juice
- 1/4 cup white wine
- 12 ounces broccoli florets
- ¼ cup sliced almonds
- 1 tbsp. Of minced ginger

Instructions:
1. Cook rice.
2. Spot four salmon filets in a heating dish.
3. In a small bowl, combine butter, curry powder, and salt.
4. Add white wine and lemon juice to the preparing dish. Cook in the microwave until salmon is cooked.

5. Blend broccoli florets, water, minced ginger, and salt together in a bowl.
6. Take the salmon out of the microwave when done. Add the broccoli; cook for almost four minutes.
7. Mix one-fourth cup cut almonds into the rice.
8. Serve rice with cooked salmon and broccoli.

2.20 Shrimp and Zucchini Scampi

Preparation Time: 20 minutes
Cooking Time: 20 minutes
Serving: 4

Ingredients:

- 2 tbsp. unsalted butter
- 1 pound of medium shrimp
- 3 minced cloves garlic
- 1/2 tsp. red pepper flakes
- 1/4 cup of chicken stock
- 1 lime
- Kosher salt, to taste
- Black pepper, to taste
- 1 1/2 pounds of zucchini
- 2 tbsp. Parmesan
- 2 tbsp. chopped parsley leaves

Instructions:
1. Heat butter in a skillet over medium-high flame. Add garlic, shrimp, and red pepper chips. Cook until pink, around two to three minutes.
2. Add chicken stock and lemon juice; season with salt and pepper to taste. Bring it to a boil; mix zucchini noodles, around one to two minutes.
3. Add parsley and Parmesan, and serve.

2.21 French-Inspired Tuna Nicoise

Preparation Time: 10 minutes
Cooking Time: 20 minutes
Serving: 2

Ingredients:

- 8 potatoes
- 4 ounces of green beans
- 2 tomatoes
- ½ cos lettuce
- 3 eggs
- 100g of black olives
- 8 to 10 ounces of chunk tuna

For Lemon Nicoise Dressing:

- 1 1/2 tbsp. of lemon juice
- 4 tbsp. olive oil
- 1 minced garlic clove
- 1/4 tsp. of salt
- 1 tsp. of Dijon mustard
- 1 black pepper Black mustard seeds, one teaspoon

Instructions:

1. Boil potatoes until delicate, set aside. Cut into equal parts.

2. Boil green beans until delicate or done as you would prefer.
3. Put cos leaves on a huge plate.
4. Mix all ingredients of Lemon Nicoise Dressing.
5. Dissipate and layer the ingredients around the plate.
6. Add eggs, olives, and lumps of fish.
7. Top with dressing and serve!

2.22 One Pan Mustard Glazed Salmon

Preparation Time: 15 minutes
Cooking Time: 15 minutes
Serving: 2

Ingredients:

- 1 thinly sliced lemon
- 1/2 lemon
- 1 ½ tbsp. grainy mustard
- 1/4 cup of chopped fresh dill
- Kosher salt, to taste
- 1 1/2 tbsp. dijon mustard
- Black pepper, to taste
- 1 2- a pound of filet steelhead
- 1 pounds of new potatoes
- 1 pound of asparagus

- 4 to 6 cloves of garlic peeled
- 2 tbsp. olive oil

Instructions:
1. Preheat the stove to 450° F.
2. Put lemon cuts on the dish.
3. In a small bowl, blend grainy mustard, lemon juice, and dijon mustard together.
4. Add pepper and salt, one teaspoon of the new dill.
5. Put salmon on dish and rub it with the mustard sauce—season with legitimate salt and dark pepper.
6. Meagerly cut the potatoes and place them in a bowl with the asparagus and crushed garlic cloves.
7. Shower with olive oil, season with pepper and salt.
8. Cook vegetables and salmon for fifteen to twenty minutes.
9. Present with mustard sauce, add more lemon wedges and serve.

2.23 Grilled Stuffed Rainbow Trout

Preparation Time: 20 minutes
Cooking Time: 20 minutes
Serving: 4

Ingredients:

- 1 halved lemon
- 5 tbsp. olive oil
- 12 chopped cloves garlic
- ¼ cup fresh thyme
- ¼ cup of fresh rosemary
- 1 tbsp. red pepper flakes
- 4 whole trout
- Pinch of salt and black pepper

Instructions:
1. Add lemon, olive oil, garlic, thyme, rosemary, and red pepper drops in a bowl.
2. Rub trout with salt and pepper. Add the lemon-spice blend in it, and place it in cooler for one hour.
3. Preheat a microwave on medium-high heat and softly oil the mesh.
4. Flame broiled trout for around four minutes for each side. Serve with lemon wedges.

2.24 Salmon and Beets with Yogurt Sauce over Watercress

Preparation Time: 10 minutes

Cooking Time: 20 minutes

Serving: 2

Ingredients:

- 1 1/4 lb. Of beets
- 1/2 cup plain yogurt
- 2 tbsp. Dill, chopped
- 1/2 tsp. Of lemon zest
- 1 tbsp. Of olive oil
- 1 tbsp. Of poppy seeds
- Kosher salt, to taste
- Black pepper, to taste
- 4 salmon fillets
- 1 tsp. Of ground coriander
- 1 bunch of watercress

Instructions:

1. Take water in a medium pan. Steam beets until delicate, for eighteen to twenty minutes.
2. In the meantime, whisk together yogurt, dill, lemon zing and juice, oil, and poppy seeds in a bowl—season with salt and pepper.

3. Preheat the grill. Cook on a rimmed heating sheet, five to six minutes.
4. Serve salmon, beets, and watercress.
5. Add yogurt sauce.

2.25 Lobster-Noodle Casserole

Preparation Time: 30 minutes
Cooking Time: 40 minutes
Serving: 8

Ingredients:

- 2 lobsters
- 2 tsp. lemon juice
- For the Cheese and Macaroni:
- 8 ounces of elbow macaroni
- 3 tbsp. Of butter
- 3 tbsp. flour
- 1 tsp. salt
- 1/8 tsp. pepper
- 1 1/2 cups of milk
- 1 cup cheddar cheese
- 1 tsp. dry mustard
- 1 1/2 cups of frozen peas
- Black pepper, to taste
- 2 tbsp. of melted butter

Instructions:
1. Heat three to four quarts of water to the point of boiling in a stockpot. Put lobsters into the water. Cover the dish.
2. Cook the lobsters for around eight minutes.
3. Break the shells and take out the meat.
4. Cleave the meat and put it in a bowl; add two teaspoons of lemon juice.
5. Preheat the stove to 400^0 F.
6. Cook the elbow macaroni in a huge pot of salted water.
7. Add flour in the butter.
8. Add one teaspoon of salt and pepper. Keep on cooking for two minutes.
9. Steadily add the milk. Keep on cooking until the sauce thickens and bubbles for one minute.
10. Spoon around half cup of the sauce over the lobster, blend tenderly.
11. Pour remaining sauce over the cooked and depleted macaroni; add the cheddar and mustard and mix.
12. Spoon the macaroni and lobster combination into the pre-arranged preparing dish; top with the lobster blend.
13. Add breadcrumbs with two tablespoons of butter. Sprinkle pieces over the meal.
14. Cover and prepare at 400 F for around twenty minutes.
15. Then, steam the peas as coordinated on the package and season with spread and salt and pepper.

16. Spoon the steamed prepared peas around the edge of the goulash not long prior to serving.

2.26 Lobster Mac and Cheese Recipe

Preparation Time: 10 minutes
Cooking Time: 20 minutes
Serving: 2

Ingredients:

- 4 tbsp. butter
- 2 tbsp. flour
- 2 1/2 cups of water
- 4 cups of milk
- 1 pound of corkscrew pasta
- 3/4 tsp. salt
- 1/4 tsp. garlic powder
- 1/4 tsp. onion powder
- 1/2 tsp. smoked paprika
- 1/4 tsp. pepper
- 4 cups of cheddar cheese
- 1 cup mozzarella cheese
- 1 1/2 cups of cooked lobster to garnish
- 1/2 cup of panko breadcrumbs
- 2 tbsp. chives

- Cooking spray

Instructions:

1. Preheat the broiler to 350 degrees F. Coat a two to three quart preparing dish with a cooking spray.
2. Soften two tablespoons of the butter in a pot over medium heat. Add the flour, cook for around thirty seconds.
3. Add water and milk.
4. Mix in the pasta, salt, garlic powder, onion powder, smoked paprika, and pepper.
5. Cook for ten to twelve minutes.
6. Turn the heat to low, add cheeses.
7. Overlap in the lobster meat. Move the pasta combination to the pre-arranged heating dish.
8. Add two tablespoons of butter into the panko breadcrumbs.
9. Sprinkle the breadcrumbs. Cook for ten to fifteen minutes.
10. Sprinkle with chives and serve.

2.27 Lemon-Parmesan Angel Hair Pasta with Shrimp

Preparation Time: 30 minutes
Cooking Time: 10 minutes
Serving: 4

Ingredients:

- 1 1/4 lbs. of shrimp
- 12 ounces of pasta
- 3 tbsp. of olive oil
- 3 Tbsp. of unsalted butter
- Salt, to taste
- Black pepper, to taste
- 3 cloves garlic
- 1 1/2 tsp. of lemon zest
- 3 tbsp. of lemon juice
- 3 tbsp. of fresh basil, chopped
- 3 tbsp. fresh parsley, chopped
- 1/2 cup of Parmesan

Instructions:
1. Cook pasta in salted water.
2. In a skillet, heat butter and olive over medium-high heat. Add shrimp, pepper, salt, and sauté for two minutes and add garlic and sauté until

shrimp has cooked through, around two minutes longer.
3. Put pasta in shrimp alongside one-third cup saved pasta water, lemon, and lemon juice.
4. Add more water one tablespoon at once. Add two tablespoons of parsley and basil, sprinkle parmesan cheddar, and serve warm.

2.28 Sheet Pan Shrimp with Broccoli and Tomatoes

Preparation Time: 30 minutes

Cooking Time: 10 minutes

Serving: 4

Ingredients:

- 1 pound of extra shrimp
- 2 tbsp. of olive oil
- 3 minced garlic cloves
- 3/4 tsp. kosher salt
- 1/8 tsp. red pepper
- Black pepper, to taste
- Olive oil
- 12 ounces of broccoli
- 1 cup of grape tomatoes
- 1 tsp. of fresh oregano
- 2 tbsp. lemon juice

Instructions:
1. Preheat the stove to 400°F.
2. Spot shrimp in a medium bowl with two teaspoons olive oil, garlic, one-fourth teaspoon salt, and pepper.
3. Shower a huge sheet skillet with olive oil.
4. Place broccoli and tomatoes in the dish.
5. Add two tablespoons olive oil, half teaspoon salt, pepper, and oregano.
6. Spread out in an even layer. Broil for fifteen minutes.
7. Get the sheet dish out of the stove and add shrimp, setting them uniformly around the veggies. Broil for eight minutes.
8. Top everything with lemon juice and serve.

2.29 Garlic Butter Shrimp

Preparation Time: 10 minutes
Cooking Time: 10 minutes
Serving: 4

Ingredients:

- 8 tablespoons of unsalted butter
- 1 1/2 pounds of medium shrimp
- Kosher salt, to taste
- Black pepper, to taste
- 5 minced cloves garlic
- 1/4 cup of chicken stock
- 1 lemon
- 2 tbsp. parsley leaves

Instructions:

1. Add shrimp, salt and pepper, to taste in the oil. Cook for around two to three minutes.
2. Add garlic to the skillet, and cook while mixing continuously until fragrant.
3. Add chicken stock and lemon juice for around 1 to 2 minutes.
4. Add six tablespoons of butter.
5. Add shrimp.
6. Add parsley leaves, and serve.

2.30 Grilled Lobster Tails with Herb Garlic Butter

Preparation Time: 10 minutes
Cooking Time: 30 minutes
Serving: 2

Ingredients:

- 3 lobster tails
- Lemon wedges
- For the butter:
- 125g butter
- 1 crushed garlic clove
- Parsley leaves, to serve
- 1 tsp. of Dijon mustard
- 1 pinch of chilli powder
- 1 lemon

Instructions:
1. Use kitchen scissors to cut along the highest points of the lobster shells, flip the tails over and break the ribs of the shell.
2. Utilize your fingers to open the shell and slacken the meat keeping it joined at the base and haul it half out.

3. Cook the lobster tails for ten minutes. Put them on a plate.
4. Present with lemon wedges and parsley.

2.31 Salmon with Chickpeas and Spinach

Preparation Time: 5 minutes
Cooking Time: 18 minutes
Serving: 4

Ingredients:

- 4 Salmon Fillets
- 4 tbsp. olive oil
- ½ tsp. kosher salt
- 2 cans of chickpeas
- ¼ tbsp. Black peppers
- 3 cloves of garlic
- 5 ounces of spinach
- 1 tsp. paprika
- 2 tsp. balsamic vinegar

Instructions:

1. Season salmon with pepper and salt.

2. Cook salmon in olive oil for around six to nine minutes.
3. Drain chickpeas.
4. Take out the salmon fillets.
5. Add more olive oil in the pan.
6. Add paprika and garlic.
7. Add chickpeas, tomatoes, kosher salt, and black pepper. Cook for five minutes.
8. Add spinach. Cook for two minutes.
9. Add vinegar.
10. Season with pepper and salt.
11. Add salmon in the pan.
12. Serve it with spinach and chickpeas.

Chapter 3: Healthy Fish and Seafood Snacks and Salads Recipes

Pescatarian seafood snacks and salads recipes are well known throughout the world. Everyone should include these yummy recipes in their Pescatarian diet plan. Here are some of these recipes given below:

3.1 Crab Cakes

Preparation Time: 10 minutes

Cooking Time: 30 minutes

Serving: 8

Ingredients:

- 1/3 cup of mayonnaise
- 1 beaten egg
- 2 tbsp. Of Dijon mustard
- 2 tsp. Of Worcestershire sauce
- 1/2 tsp. Of hot sauce
- Kosher salt, to taste
- Black pepper
- 1 lb. Of crabmeat
- 3/4 cup of breadcrumbs
- 2 tbsp. Chopped Parsley
- Canola oil, to fry
- Lemon wedges, to serve

- Tartar sauce, to serve

Instructions:
1. In a small bowl, whisk together egg, mayo, Dijon mustard, hot sauce, Worcestershire, and season with pepper and salt.
2. In a medium bowl, mix together crabmeat, panko, and parsley.
3. Make eight patties.
4. In a skillet over medium heat, cover the container with oil and heat until shining. Add crab cakes and cook for three to five minutes.
5. Present with lemon and tartar sauce.

3.2 Shrimp Ceviche

Preparation Time: 5 minutes
Cooking Time: 30 minutes
Serving: 6

Ingredients:

- 1/2 cup of thinly sliced red
- 1 jalapeno
- 2 pounds of cooked shrimp cooked
- 3/4 cup of diced cucumber
- 1 cup of diced Roma tomatoes
- 3/4 cup of chopped cilantro leaves
- 1 chopped avocado peeled
- 1/2 cup of lime juice
- 1/4 cup lemon juice
- Salt, to taste
- 1/3 cup orange juice
- Tortilla chips to serve

Instructions:

1. Put the shrimp, jalapeno, red onion, cucumber, avocado, and cilantro in a bowl.

2. Pour the lime, lemon, and squeezed orange on the shrimp.

3. Add salt.

4. Refrigerate for up to eight hours. Serve with tortilla chips.

3.3 Salmon Patties

Preparation Time: 10 minutes
Cooking Time: 20 minutes
Serving: 5

Ingredients:

- 1 of diced can salmon
- 2 thinly sliced green onions
- 1 tbsp. Of fresh dill, chopped
- 1/2 cup of panko bread crumbs
- 1/4 cup of Mayonnaise
- 1 tbsp. lemon juice
- 1 tbsp. Of Dijon mustard
- 1 beaten egg
- kosher salt, to taste
- Black pepper, to taste
- 2 tbsp. Of olive oil,
- Baby spinach, to serve

Instructions:

1. In a bowl, add ingredients—season with salt and pepper and blend.

2. Structure into five equally measured patties. Cook patties in clusters until brilliant and fresh, three to four minutes for every side.
3. Serve over spinach with lemon wedges.

3.4: Crab Hush Puppies

Preparation Time: 20 minutes
Cooking Time: 12 minutes
Serving: 8

Ingredients:

- 1 cup of yellow cornmeal
- 1/2 cup of flour
- 1 tbsp. sugar
- 1/2 tsp. salt
- 1/2 tsp. Creole seasoning
- 1/2 tsp. onion powder
- 1/4 tsp. baking powder
- 1/4 tsp. baking soda
- 1/2 cup of finely diced bell pepper, red
- 3 diced, green onions
- 1 lightly beaten egg
- 1/4 cup of buttermilk
- 1/2 cup of beer
- 8 ounces of crab meat
- Vegetable oil, as required
- For Remoulade Sauce:
- 3/4 cup of mayonnaise
- 1 1/2 tbsp. Creole mustard

- 1 tsp. horseradish
- 2 sliced green onions
- 1 tbsp. fresh parsley, chopped
- 1 minced garlic clove

Instructions:
1. Start by making the Remoulade sauce.
2. Mix all ingredients in a bowl and refrigerate.
3. In a huge bowl, mix together cornmeal, flour, sugar, salt, Creole flavoring, onion powder, preparing powder, red pepper and green onions.
4. Add the egg, buttermilk, and brew and mix to blend.
5. Tenderly blend in crab meat. Let sit for ten minutes.
6. Heat oven to 360 degrees.
7. Working in bunches, fry for two to three minutes.
8. Keep warm in a 200 degrees broiler.
9. Present with sauce.

3.5 Baked Clams

Preparation Time: 30 minutes
Cooking Time: 20
Serving: 6-8

Ingredients:

- 10-12 chowder clams
- 3 tbsp. minced onion
- 1/2 cup of butter
- 2 tbsp. fresh parsley chopped
- 1 minced clove garlic
- 1 tbsp. lemon juice
- 1 cup of breadcrumbs
- 1tbsp. clam juice
- Pepper, to taste
- Salt, o taste of
- 1/4 cup of Parmesan cheese

Instructions:

1. Fill a huge pot with half cup of water. Heat water to the point of boiling. Add the shellfishes to the bubbling water.

2. Let the mollusks steam for roughly six to ten minutes until the shells open.
3. Take mollusks out of the pot.
4. Preheat broiler to 350°F. In a sauté dish, add the minced onion. Cook for two to three minutes.
5. Add garlic.
6. Cook the garlic, add the parsley, bread scraps, minced mollusks, lemon juice, and shellfish juice.
7. Lay shellfish shells on a dish. Scoop a little stuffing blend onto each shellfish shell.
8. Sprinkle with ground Parmesan.
9. Prepare at 350°F for around twenty to twenty-five minutes until Parmesan is daintily sautéed on top.

3.6 General Tso's Shrimp 'n Broccoli

Preparation Time: 20 minutes
Cooking Time: 20 minutes
Serving: 4

Ingredients:

- 4 20 20
- 1 grated clove garlic
- 3 tbsp. Of soy sauce
- 2 tbsp. Of white vinegar
- 2 tbsp. Of sugar
- 1/3 cup ketchup
- 1/2 tsp. Of dry mustard
- 1 head broccoli
- 1 lb. Of shrimp
- Black pepper, to taste
- Kosher salt, to taste
- 1/2 cup cornstarch
- Vegetable oil, to fry
- 1 tbsp. Of sesame seeds

Instructions:

1. Put together garlic, soy sauce, vinegar, sugar, ketchup, and mustard in a skillet. Heat to the point of boiling.
2. Steam broccoli in a pot.
3. In the meantime, in a medium blending bowl, season shrimp with salt and pepper.
4. Dig shrimp in cornstarch.
5. Preheat a huge skillet over medium-high heat with 1/2" of oil and cook.
6. Spoon sauce over shrimp and sautéed food until caramelized.
7. Serve on top of steamed broccoli and topped with sesame seeds.

3.7 Bang Bang Shrimp

Preparation Time: 10 minutes

Cooking Time: 10 minutes

Serving: 4

Ingredients:

- 1/2 cup of mayonnaise
- 1/4 cup of chili sauce, Thai sweet
- 1/4 tsp. Sriracha
- 1 pound of shrimp shelled

- 1/2 cup of buttermilk
- 3/4 cup of cornstarch
- Canola oil, to fry

Instructions:
1. In a small bowl, add the mayonnaise, Thai sweet stew sauce, and Sriracha and mix.
2. In another bowl, add the shrimp and buttermilk.
3. Coat the shrimp in cornstarch.
4. In a hefty lined dish, add two to three creeps of canola oil and heat to 375 degrees.
5. Fry the shrimp until daintily earthy colored, one to two minutes on each side.
6. Coat with sauce and serve.

3.8 Simple Ceviche Recipe

Preparation Time: 15 minutes
Cooking Time: 15 minutes
Serving: 8

Ingredients:

- 1 pound of cooked shrimp
- ¼ cup of lemon juice
- ¼ cup of fresh lime juice
- ½ cup of fresh orange juice
- 4 diced plum tomatoes seeds
- 2 minced jalapeno peppers
- 1 cup of diced jicama
- ½ cup of chopped cilantro
- ¼ cup of finely chopped red onion
- 1 diced avocado
- Black pepper, to taste
- Kosher salt, to taste

Instructions:
1. Cut out the shrimp into half inch pieces and move to a bowl.
2. Mix the lemon, lime, and squeezed orange to join.
3. Pour citrus juice over the shrimp.

4. Permit the shrimp to marinate for fifteen minutes.
5. Add the jalapeño, tomato, jicama (or apple), red onion, and cilantro to the shrimp.
6. Mix the ingredients and left to marinade for an extra ten minutes.
7. Add avocado and the remaining juices.
8. Add pepper and salt. Serve quickly with tortilla chips.

3.9 Smoked Salmon, Avocado, and Fennel Salad

Preparation Time: 15 minutes
Cooking Time: 15
Serving: 2

Ingredients:

- ⅓ cup of mayo
- 1 tbsp. Of olive oil
- 1/3 cup of sour cream
- 2 tbsp. Of lemon juice
- 1/3 cup of chopped fresh dill
- 1/4 tsp. Salt
- 2 minced garlic cloves
- Salad (2 servings)
- 1/4 tsp. Of cracked pepper
- 1 head of butter lettuce
- 1 Turkish sliced cucumber
- 1/2 thinly sliced fennel bulb
- 4 to 6 ounces of smoked salmon
- ⅛ cup of red onion, thinly sliced
- 2 tbsp. capers
- 1 sliced avocado
- Sunflower sprouts

Instructions:

1. Place ingredients for dressing in a bowl and race until smooth, and blend in dill.
2. Add fennel bulb, lettuce, cucumber, red onion, tricks, and smoked salmon in a major bowl.
3. You can either prepare avocado and fledglings now or separate the serving of mixed greens.
4. Add avocado, sprinkle with pepper and salt, and serve.

3.10 Cilantro-Lime Shrimp Salad

Preparation Time: 10 minutes

Cooking Time: 10 minutes

Serving: 2

Ingredients:

- 1/4 cup red onion
- 2 limes
- 1 tsp. Olive oil
- ¼ tsp. Of Black pepper
- 1/4 tsp. kosher salt
- 1 lb. jumbo cooked
- 1 tomato, diced
- 1 avocado, diced

- 1 jalapeno, diced
- 1 tbsp. chopped cilantro

Instructions:

1. Put the lime juice, red onion, olive oil, pepper, and salt in a small bowl. Allow them to marinate for five minutes.

2. In a bowl, join slashed avocado, shrimp, tomato, and jalapeño.

3. Add cilantro, pepper, and salt to taste.

3.11 Shrimp Salad

Preparation Time: 5 minutes
Cooking Time: 10 minutes
Serving: 2

Ingredients:

- 1 lb. of shrimp
- 1 tbsp. Of olive oil
- Black pepper
- Kosher salt
- 1/4 of chopped red onion
- 1 chopped stalk celery
- 2 tbsp. Of chopped dill
- Butterhead, to serve

FOR DRESSING

- 1 lemon
- 1/2 cup mayonnaise
- 1 tsp. Of dijon mustard

Instructions:
1. Preheat stove to 400°F. On a heating sheet, throw shrimp with oil and season with salt and pepper.
2. Prepare until shrimp are dark, five to seven minutes.

3. Add mayonnaise, zest, and juice of lemon, Dijon, pepper, and salt in a bowl. Add shrimp, celery, dill, and red onion to a bowl and throw until consolidated.
4. Serve on bread or over lettuce.

3.12 Smoked Salmon and Oatmeal Salad

Preparation Time: 15 minutes
Cooking Time: 20 minutes
Serving: 4

Ingredients:

- 4 onions
- 6 diced tomatoes
- 1 diced ripe avocado
- 2 red chilli
- 1 lime,
- 3 tbsp. of wood chips
- 600g salmon fillets
- 3 tsp. Of rapeseed oil
- 125g of oatmeal

Instructions:
1. To start with, make the salsa.
2. Finely slash the green highest points of the spring onions. Blend in tomatoes, the avocado, and half

bean stew, and lime zest. Season and put away to marinate.

3. Brush the salmon with the rapeseed oil and spot it on the rack.

4. Cook on a BBQ or on a hob for eight to ten minutes. Keep warm.

5. For the oats, heat the leftover rapeseed oil in a griddle and fry the whites of the spring onions for one to two minutes.

6. Add the oats and cook for three to four minutes. Mix in one hundred and fifty ml water and lime juice.

7. Cushion it up with a fork and add any leftover tomatoes.

8. Serve the salmon fillets, salsa and oats.

3.13 Pan Seared Scallops and Quinoa Salad

Preparation Time: 25 minutes
Cooking Time: 20 minutes
Serving: 2

Ingredients:

- 1 cup of white or red quinoa
- 1 1/2 cups of water
- Kosher salt, to taste
- 1 tbsp. Of olive oil
- 2-4 tbsp. Fresh basil
- Ground pepper, to taste
- 2 oranges
- 1 finely diced avocado
- 3 tbsp. fresh basil
- 2 tbsp. minced shallot
- 1 1/2 tsp. minced red jalapeño
- Kosher salt, to taste
- Black pepper, to taste
- 2 tbsp. olive oil
- 10-12 ounces of sea scallops

Instructions:
1. To make the quinoa, place the quinoa in a pan, wash with cold water.

2. Add half cup of water and salt and heat to the point of boiling around 15 minutes.
3. Cushion the quinoa with a fork.
4. Add olive oil and basil.
5. Season with pepper and salt.
6. Cut the oranges down the middle, cut them into slices.
7. Add avocado, shallot, jalapeño, basil, pepper, and salt.
8. In a fry pan, over medium-high heat, heat olive oil. Season the scallops with pepper and salt, and sauté until practically springy to the touch, around two minutes for each side.
9. Spread the quinoa on two plates. Top with the salsa and scallops and serve.

3.14 Shrimp and Avocado Taco Salad

Preparation Time: 20 minutes
Cooking Time: 15 minutes
Serving: 2

Ingredients:

- 2 tbsp. oil
- 1 lb. Of medium shrimp
- 1 head of chopped romaine lettuce
- 4 diced tomatoes
- ½ finely diced jalapeño
- ¼ finely diced red onion
- 2 tbsp. Minced fresh cilantro
- 1 large diced avocado
- ½ tsp. salt
- 2 tbsp. lime juice
- For Taco Seasoning
- ½ tsp. salt
- ½ tsp. black pepper
- 1 tsp. ground cumin
- 1 tsp. dried oregano
- ¼ tsp. garlic powder
- ½ tsp. chili powder

Instructions:

1. Add shrimp and season with the taco. Sauté the shrimp just until each piece has begun to become pink.
2. In a huge bowl, put lettuce, shrimp, tomatoes, jalapeño, red onion, cilantro, avocado, salt, and lime squeeze.
3. Present with tortilla strips, and serve.

3.15 Crab and Shrimp Salad with Mango

Preparation Time: 15 minutes
Cooking Time: 20 minutes
Serving: 4

Ingredients:

For Yuzu vinaigrette:
- 2 yuzus, shredded zest
- 1 1/2 tbsp. of yuzu juice
- 1/4 tsp. kosher salt
- 1/8 tsp. Of fresh black pepper
- 1/4 cup of fruity olive oil
- For Soy-ginger mayo:
- 1 tsp. fresh ginger
- 1/3 cup of mayonnaise
- 1 tsp. soy sauce
- 1 1/2 tbsp. yuzu juice

For Salad:
- 2 mangoes
- 1/2 pound of cooked crab
- 1/2 pound of tiny shrimp
- 5 ounces of baby arugula
- 4 lime leaves

Instructions:

1. Make the vinaigrette: In a medium bowl, put lemon zest.
2. Add salt and pepper.
3. Add olive oil.
4. In a small bowl, mix all mayo ingredients.
5. Cut mangoes.
6. In a medium bowl, mix crab and shrimp with two tablespoons of vinaigrette.
7. In another bowl, blend mangoes and arugula with the remaining vinaigrette.
8. Top with crab combination. Sprinkle with lime leaves.
9. Serve and enjoy.

3.16 Shoyu Ahi Poke Recipe

Preparation Time: 10 minutes
Cooking Time: 10 minutes
Serving: 4

Ingredients:

- 4 10 10
- 1 pound of ahi
- ¼ cup of green onions
- ¼ cup of sweet onion
- 2 tbsp. shoyu
- 1 tsp. Of sesame oil

Instructions:
1. Cut ahi into pieces.
2. Cut sweet and green onions.
3. Add ahi, green onion, sweet onion, shoyu, and sesame oil to a blending bowl.
4. Tenderly mix to consolidate.
5. Serve and enjoy.

Chapter 4: Healthy Fish and Seafood Soup Recipes

Pescatarian fish and seafood soup recipes provide plenty of health benefits. They keep you full and also fulfill your nutritional requirements. Try the following recipes at home:

4.1 Lobster Bisque

Preparation Time: 20 minutes
Cooking Time: 55 minutes
Serving: 3

Ingredients:

- For Bisque
- 2 tablespoons butter
- 3 lobster tails
- 1 tbsp. olive oil
- 1 finely chopped onion
- 2 finely chopped carrots
- 2 finely chopped stalks of celery
- 1 tsp. chopped thyme
- 1 tsp. chopped tarragon
- 1 tsp. bouillon powder, chicken
- 1/2 tsp. salt

- 1/4 tsp. fresh black pepper
- 1/2 tsp. cayenne pepper
- 4 minced cloves garlic
- 2 tbsp. tomato paste
- 3 tbsp. flour
- 1 1/4 cup of white wine
- 4 cups of lobster stock
- 3/4 - 1 cup of heavy cream
- For Garlic Butter Lobster Meat
- 2 tbsp. butter
- 2 minced cloves garlic
- Pepper, to taste
- Salt, to taste
- Pepper, to taste

Instructions:

1. Fill a huge pot with five cups of water. Mix in one tsp. sea salt and heat to the point of boiling.
2. Add the lobster tails, cover with top and let bubble for five minutes, or until radiant red.
3. Eliminate lobster tails.
4. Set aside the fluid stock. When the lobsters are cool somewhat, eliminate the meat from the shells, saving the meat and any fluid that emerges from the shells.
5. Cook to the point of boiling, diminish heat to low and cook for a further fifteen minutes.
6. While the stock is stewing, cut meat into pieces and refrigerate.

7. Heat oil and butter in a pot over medium heat.
8. Add carrots, onions, new spices, and celery. Cook until delicate, around five minutes.
9. Season with the bouillon powder, pepper, and salt.
10. Mix in minced garlic and cook until fragrant, around one minute.
11. Blend in tomato glue, cook briefly to cover vegetables. Sprinkle over the flour and cook for a further two minutes.
12. Pour the wine and cook. Mix in lobster stock, lessen the heat and cook while mixing periodically until the fluid has thickened and flavors have mixed around thirty minutes.
13. Remove the heat, transfer the mixture to a blender, and mix until smooth. Then again, purée with a blender until extremely smooth. Get back to medium-low heat and add cream.
14. Dissolve the butter in a skillet over medium heat. Sauté garlic for around thirty seconds, until fragrant. Add lobster meat, season with salt, pepper, and cayenne to taste. Gently sauté for one minute.
15. Blend three-fourth of the lobster meat into the bisque. Fill serving bowls.
16. Top each bowl with lobster meat.

4.2 Italian Fish Stew

Preparation Time: 20 minutes
Cooking Time: 45 minutes
Serving: 4

Ingredients:

- 8 ounces of fresh sea bass fillets
- 6 ounces of medium shrimp
- ⅓ cup of chopped onion
- 2 sliced stalks celery
- ½ tsp. minced garlic
- 2 tsp. olive oil
- 1 cup of chicken broth
- ¼ cup of white wine
- 1 can of diced tomatoes
- 1 can of tomato sauce
- 1 tsp. Crushed dried oregano
- ¼ tsp. salt
- ⅛ tsp. Black pepper
- 1 tbsp. fresh parsley

Instructions:

1. Defrost fish and shrimp. Wash fish and shrimp; wipe off with paper towels.

2. Cut fish into one-inch pieces. Slice shrimp.
3. Cover and chill fish and shrimp until required.
4. In a huge pot, cook onion, garlic, and celery in hot oil. Add one cup of stock and wine. Cook for five minutes.
5. Add tomatoes, oregano, pepper, and salt, and pepper. Cook for five minutes.
6. Add fish and shrimp. Lower the heat. Cook for three to five minutes.
7. Sprinkle with parsley, and serve.

4.3 Asian Shrimp and Vegetable Soup

Preparation Time: 15 minutes
Cooking Time: 35 minutes
Serving: 4

Ingredients:

- 12 ounces of large shrimp
- 4 onions
- 2 tsp. canola oil
- 2 thinly sliced carrots
- 8 ounces of oyster mushrooms
- 1 tbsp. Of fresh ginger
- 2 minced cloves garlic
- 2 cans of chicken broth
- 2 cups of water
- 1 cup of sweet soybeans
- 1 tbsp. soy sauce
- ¼ tsp. red pepper
- 1 cup of peas
    - 1 Hot onion sauce
    - Feta cheese

Instructions:

1. Defrost frozen shrimp. Wash shrimp and wipe off with paper towels.

2. Cut green onions into one-inch-long pieces, keeping white parts separate from green tops.
3. In a nonstick pan, heat oil over medium flame. Add white pieces of carrots, green onions, and mushrooms; cook for about five minutes.
4. Add garlic.
5. Add water, chicken stock, soybeans, and soy sauce, crushed red pepper, and mushroom blend.
6. Wait for it to boil, lessen the heat. Cook for around five minutes.
7. Add shrimp and pea pods to the pan. Cook for two to three minutes or until shrimp are murky.
8. Put green onion beat in it not long prior to serving. Decorate with fragmented green onions.

4.4 Salmon Chowder

Preparation Time: 15 minutes
Cooking Time: 15 minutes
Serving: 4

Ingredients:

- 3 tbsp. butter
- ¾ cup of chopped onion
- ½ cup of chopped celery
- 1 tsp. garlic powder
- 2 cups of diced potatoes
- 2 diced carrots
- 2 cups of chicken broth
- 1 tsp. salt
- 1 tsp. black pepper
- 1 tsp. dill weed
- 2 cans of salmon
- 1 can of evaporated milk
- 1 can of creamed corn
- ½ pound of shredded Cheddar cheese

Instructions:

1. Heat butter in a pot over medium heat. Sauté onion, garlic powder, and celery.

2. Put dill potatoes, pepper, stock, carrots, salt, and pepper in it.
3. Heat to the point of boiling, then cook for twenty minutes.
4. Add salmon, vanished milk, corn, and cheddar. Cook until warmed through, and serve.

4.5 Seafood Cioppino

Preparation Time: 45 minutes
Cooking Time: 2 hrs. 15 mins
Serving: 4

Ingredients:

- ¼ cup of olive oil
- 1 chopped onion
- 4 minced cloves garlic
- One chopped bell pepper, green
- 1 chopped red chile pepper
- ½ cup of chopped parsley
- Pepper, to taste
- Salt, to taste
- 1 tsp. Dried oregano
- 1 tsp. dried thyme
- ½ cup of water
- 1 can of crushed tomatoes
- 2 tsp. dried basil
- 1 can of tomato sauce
- 1 pinch of paprika
- 1 pinch of cayenne pepper
- 25 shrimp
- 1 cup of white wine

- 1 can of minced clams
- 25 mussels
- 10 ounces of scallops
- 1 pound cubed cod fillets

Instructions:

1. Sauté the onion, pepper, garlic, pepper, and chile pepper in the oil.
2. Add parsley, pepper and salt, basil, thyme, oregano, tomatoes, water, pureed tomatoes, paprika, and cayenne pepper; squeeze from the shellfishes. Mix well, diminish heat, and cook for one to two hours.
3. Add wine.
4. Around ten minutes prior to serving, add mollusks, cod, prawns, mussels, and scallops.
5. Turn on the heat and mix.
6. Serve your tasty cioppino.

4.6 Wild Rice, Shrimp & Fennel Soup

Preparation Time: 30 minutes
Cooking Time: 40 minutes
Serving: 6

Ingredients:

- 1 pound shrimp
- 1 fennel bulb
- 1 tbsp. olive oil
- 1 tbsp. unsalted butter
- 1 cup of leeks
- 1 carrot
- ¾ cup of uncooked rice
- ¼ tsp. Salt
- ¼ tsp. ground pepper
- 2 cans of chicken broth
- 1 cup of water
- ¾ cup milk
- 2 tbsp. flour
- 2 tsp. fresh thyme
- 2 tbsp. dry sherry
- 1 sprig of thyme sprigs

Instructions:
1. Defrost frozen shrimp.
2. Heat butter and oil in a pot over medium heat.
3. Add the slashed fennel, carrot, and leeks; cook for around eight minutes or until delicate.
4. Mix in wild rice, pepper, and salt. Cook and add stock and water. Bring it to boil; diminish heat. Cover it and cook for forty five minutes.
5. Whisk together milk and flour in a small bowl. Whisk the milk blend into the soup alongside thyme. Cook and mix until the soup is thickened.
6. Mix the shrimp into the soup.
7. Cook for two to three minutes.
8. Add sherry.
9. Top with the fennel leaves and thyme twigs, and serve.

4.7 Seafood Stew

Preparation Time: 15 minutes
Cooking Time: 25 minutes
Serving: 4

Ingredients:

- 3 divided garlic cloves
- 2 tbsp. olive oil
- 1/2 cup of fennel
- 3/4 cup of onion
- 1 tsp. Of divided kosher salt
- 1/2 tsp. Of divided black pepper
- 1/2 pound of cleaned squid
- 1/2 tbsp. Of tomato paste
- 1/4 cup of celery
- 1 tsp. dried oregano
- 1 cup of white wine
- 1 15-ounce can of crushed tomatoes
- 3 bay leaves
- 1 bottle of clam juice
- 1/2 tsp. of red-pepper flakes
- 1 1/2 cups of seafood stock
- 1/2 stick of unsalted butter
- 3 tbsp. Of chopped parsley, divided

- 1/2 tsp. lemon zest
- 1 pound of littleneck clams
- 1/2 pound of shrimp
- 1 baguette
- 1 pound of mussels
- ½ pound of white fish

Instructions:
1. Add onion, celery, fennel, half tsp. salt, and one-fourth tsp. of pepper in the oil and cook for six to eight minutes.
2. Add red pepper flakes and garlic. Keep on cooking for one to two minutes.
3. Add oregano and tomato paste.
4. Add wine, raise heat to medium-high, and cook for five to seven minutes.
5. Add tomatoes with their juice, bay leaves, stock, and cleaned squid. Heat to the point of boiling, diminish to a stew, and cook, covered, for thirty minutes.
6. Mix in one-fourth teaspoon of each salt and pepper.
7. In the meantime, blend the butter, lemon zest, parsley, and salt together in a small bowl. Spread the seasoned butter on toasts.
8. When prepared to serve, add shellfishes; cook for almost three minutes. Mix in the mussels and shrimp.
9. It is ready. Cut into pieces; serve hot with the gremolata toasts and Taco Bell sauce.

10. You can also garnish with onions, sour cream, or cilantro.

4.8 Brazilian Fish Stew

Preparation Time: 10 minutes
Cooking Time: 25 minutes
Serving: 4

Ingredients:

- For Fish:
- 1 pound of white fish
- ½ tsp. salt
- 1 lime
- For Stew/ Sauce:
- 2–3 tbsp. Olive or coconut oil
- 1 finely diced onion- finely diced
- 1/2 tsp. salt
- 1 cup diced carrot
- 1 diced bell pepper, red
- 4 chopped garlic cloves
- ½ finely diced jalapeno
- 1 tbsp. tomato paste
- 2 tsp. paprika
- 1 tsp. ground cumin
- 1 cup of chicken stock
- 1 1/2 cups of diced tomatoes
- 1 can of coconut milk

- Salt, to taste
- ½ cup of chopped scallions
- 1 lime

Instructions:
1. Add salt, lemon zest, and one tablespoon of lime juice in the fish.
2. In a huge sauté pan, heat the olive oil over medium heat. Add onion and salt, and sauté for two to three minutes.
3. Turn heat down to medium, add carrot, chime pepper, garlic, and jalapeno and cook for four to five additional minutes.
4. Add tomato paste, flavors, and stock. Blend and cook.
5. Add tomatoes.
6. Cook for five minutes.
7. Add the coconut milk and salt.
8. Settle the fish in the stew until it is cooked for around four to six minutes.
9. Add coconut stock over the fish and cook.
10. Add lime.
11. To serve, serve over rice, sprinkle with cilantro or scallions.
12. Shower with a little olive oil. Spot one tortilla on top of the sauce in the dish, and spread a portion of the cheddar sauce on top of the tortilla. Top with the leftover vegetable sauce from the bowl.

13. Place the second tortilla on top, add cheddar sauce and blended cheddar.
14. Heat the sauce and cheddar until it is dissolved.
15. Add coriander, Serve with avocado and bean stew.

4.9 Clam Chowder

Preparation Time: 15 minutes
Cooking Time: 30 minutes
Serving: 6

Ingredients:

- 4 diced slices of bacon
- 2 tbsp. unsalted butter
- 2 minced cloves garlic
- 1 diced onion
- 1/2 tsp. dried thyme
- 3 tbsp. flour
- 1 cup of milk
- 1 cup of vegetable stock
- 2 cans of chopped clams
- 2 bay leaf
- 2 potatoes
- Kosher salt, to taste

- Black pepper, to taste
- 2 tbsp. chopped parsley leaves

Instructions:

1. Cook bacon until earthy colored and firm, around six to eight minutes.
2. Add butter, garlic and onion in a pot, and cook for around two to three minutes.
3. Mix in thyme.
4. Add flour, milk, vegetable stock, shellfish squeeze, and sound leaf, and cook, whisking continually until marginally thickened, around for one to two minutes. Put potatoes in it.
5. Cook around for twelve to fifteen minutes.
6. Mix in cream and shellfishes until warmed through.
7. Season with salt and pepper to taste.
8. Add bacon and parsley, and serve.

4.10 Crab-Okra Gumbo

Preparation Time: 15 minutes
Cooking Time: 1.30 hours
Serving: 8

Ingredients:

- 15 1.30 8
- 1 cup vegetable oil
- 1 pound diced fresh okra
- 4 tbsp. butter
- 1 cup flour
- 2 cups of yellow onion
- 1 1/2 cups of bell pepper, green
- 1/2 cup of diced celery
- 2 minced garlic cloves
- 1 can of diced tomatoes
- 4 cups of shrimp stock
- 3 bay leaves
- 1 tsp. salt
- 1 tsp. Cajun seasoning
- 1 tsp. hot sauce
- 1/2 tsp. dried thyme
- 1/2 tsp. white pepper

- 1 pound of lump crabmeat
- 2 tbsp. fresh parsley
- 1 pound of shrimp
- 1 pint of oysters

Instructions:

1. In a huge nonstick skillet, heat three tbsp. of vegetable oil over medium heat. Add okra and cook, blending every now and again for twenty-five to thirty minutes or until okra is soft.
2. Eliminate from heat and put away.
3. Heat vegetable oil in a pot.
4. Add flour and cook and mix for thirty minutes, or until a dull earthy colored tone.
5. Add onion, pepper, and celery. Cook, regularly mixing for eight minutes.
6. Add garlic and cook for two minutes.
7. Add tomatoes, stock, cove leaves, salt, Creole flavoring, hot sauce, thyme, white pepper, and okra.
8. Stew for forty five minutes.
9. Add crab meat and parsley.
10. Cook for three minutes.
11. Add shrimp and cook for almost two minutes.
12. Add shellfish and cook just until their edges begin to twist.

13. Present with rice.

4.11 Crab Bisque

Preparation Time: 10 minutes
Cooking Time: 55 minutes
Serving: 4

Ingredients:

- 3 tbsp. Of butter
- 1 finely chopped medium onion
- 2 finely chopped stalks of celery
- Kosher salt, to taste
- Black pepper, to taste
- 1 tsp. Of seasoning, Old Bay
- 2 minced cloves garlic
- 2 tbsp. Of tomato paste
- 3 tbsp. Of flour
- 4 cup fish stock
- 1 cup of dry white wine
- 3 bay leaf
- 1/2 cup of heavy cream
- 1 pound crab meat
- Chopped parsley to garnish

Instructions:

1. Add celery and onion in the butter, and cook until delicate, around five minutes.
2. Season with salt, pepper, and Old Bay. Mix garlic and tomato glue.
3. Cook until garlic is fragrant and tomato glue coats vegetables, around two minutes.
4. Sprinkle over the flour.
5. Pour in fish stock and wine; mix bay leaf. Lessen heat and let stew until fluid is decreased and seasons merge for thirty minutes.
6. Eliminate bay leaf and puree soup with a blender on high until extremely smooth.
7. Get back to medium-low heat and mix cream and half of the crab meat.
8. Cook for around five minutes.
9. Split between bowls and add crab meat and parsley before serving.

4.12 Slow-Cooked Shrimp and Scallop Soup

Preparation Time: 5minutes
Cooking Time: 3.50 hours
Serving: 6

Ingredients:

- 28 ounce of crushed tomatoes
- 1 Tbsp. tomato paste
- 4 cups of vegetable broth
- 3 minced garlic cloves
- 1 pound of yellow potatoes
- 1/2 cup of white onion
- 1 tsp. dried thyme
- 1 tsp. dried basil
- 1 tsp. Dried oregano
- 1/2 tsp. celery salt
- 1/4 tsp. crushed flakes, red pepper
- 1/8 tsp. cayenne pepper
- Pepper and salt, to taste
- 2 pounds of seafood
- Chopped parsley

Instructions:

1. Add all ingredients aside from the fish into a cooker. Cover and cook on high for two to three

hours or low for four to six hours until potatoes are cooked.
2. Add defrosted fish.
3. Cook for an hour until the fish is completely cooked.
4. Do topping with parsley. Serve hot with hard bread.

4.13 Lemon Salmon Soup

Preparation Time: 10 minutes
Cooking Time: 12 minutes
Serving: 4

Ingredients:

- Olive oil
- 4 chopped green onions
- ½ chopped bell pepper, green
- 4 minced garlic cloves
- 1 ounce fresh chopped
- 5 cups of chicken broth
- 1 pound gold potatoes
- 1 thinly sliced carrot
- 1 tsp. Of dry oregano
- ¾ tsp. coriander
- ½ tsp. cumin
- Black pepper and Kosher salt

- 1 pound salmon fillet

  1 lemon

Instructions:

1. Heat two tbsp. Olive oil in a pot. Add green onions, chile pepper, and garlic and cook over medium heat. Cook for around three minutes. Add half of the dill, and mix for thirty seconds.
2. Add stock, potatoes, and carrots. Add flavors and season with pepper and salt. Cook for five to six minutes.
3. Season salmon with salt and add it to the pot of soup. Lower heat and cook for a couple of minutes until salmon is cooked through, around three to five minutes.
4. Mix in lemon juice, lemon zest, and remaining dill.
5. Move salmon soup to serving bowls. Serve with dry bread.

Conclusion

A Pescatarian diet normally incorporates vegetables, grains, fish and seafood yet, for the most part, it avoids meat and dairy. The Pescatarian diet is broadly acknowledged similar to a nutritious decision because of the known advantages of a vegan way of life, combined with lean white fish, high-protein, and omega-3 unsaturated fats found in slick fish, including salmon, herring, and mackerel. This way of eating has shown a decreased danger of creating conditions, for example, type 2 diabetes, hypertension, and stoutness, which are all dangerous factors for coronary illness. Likewise, a recent report showed that omega-3 unsaturated fats are related to a lower hazard of lethal respiratory failures.

As per the studies, a Pescatarian diet helps to attain lower blood cholesterol levels, circulatory strain, and a lower hazard of diabetes. It also helps to treat metabolic disorders. The recipes given in **Pescatarian Cookbook** will help you achieve your desired health benefits.